Dedicated to . . .

. . . Tranmere Rovers fans everywhere!

Thanks to . . .

I should like to express my thanks to the following organisations for their help:

Tranmere Rovers FC: The Association of Football Statisticians; The Football League; The British Newspaper Library; The Harris Library, Preston; The Birkenhead Central Library; and the Local Study Libraries of Wirral and Liverpool.

Thanks also to the following individuals: Ben Hayes; Iain Price; Robert Lomas; Stephen Whittle and Cyril Walker.

Bibliography

A-Z of Tranmere Rovers (Peter Bishop) *1990*

Breedon Book of Football League Records (Gordon Smailes) 1991

Football League Archives, Handbooks

Football League Players' Records 1946-1992 (Barry Hugman) 1992

Football on Merseyside (Percy M. Young)

Rothmans Football Year Books

Three sides of the Mersey (Rogan Taylor and Andrew Ward) 1993

Tranmere Rovers 1881-1921 (Gilbert Upton)

Tranmere Rovers 1921-1997 – A Complete Record (Gilbert Upton and Steve Wilson) 1997

Tranmere Rovers programmes.

ABANDONED MATCHES

A match which is called off by the referee whilst it is in progress because conditions do not permit it to be completed. Generally speaking, far fewer matches are now abandoned because if there is some doubt about the ability to play the full game, the match is more likely to be postponed. Below is a full list of abandoned matches involving Tranmere Rovers:

Date	Opponents	Competition	Score	Reason
10.04.1924	Rochdale (H)	Div 3 (N)	2-2	Bad Light (78 mins)
26.12.1933	Wrexham (A)	Div 3 (N)	1-1	Fog (58 mins)
27.02.1937	Accrington S. (H)	Div 3 (N)	0-2	Blizzard (50 mins)
05.03.1949	Chester (H)	Div 3 (N)	0-1	Blizzard (45 mins)
19.11.1949	Doncaster R. (A)	Div 3 (N)	0-1	Fog (57 mins)
14.01.1956	Bradford PA (A)	Div 3 (N)	0-0	Fog (61 mins)
18.08.1956	Workington (H)	Div 3 (N)	0-0	Waterlogged (45mins)
23.02.1957	Darlington (H)	Div 3 (N)	0-1	Waterlogged (36mins)
06.02.1960	Grimsby T. (H)	Div 3 (N)	0-1	Fog (35 mins)
05.12.1964	Rochdale (A)	Div 4	1-0	Fog (22 mins)
28.12.1965	Notts C. (A)	Div 4	0-0	Fog (14 mins)
16.09.1980	York City (A)	Div 4	0-3	Waterlogged (48mins)
01.10.1985	Peterborough (H)	Div 4	0-1	Floodlight failure (57 mins)
19.12.1986	Hartlepool U. (H)	Div 4	0-0	Floodlight failure (27 mins)
12.12.1992	Swindon Town (A)	Div 1	2-1	Floodlight failure (50 mins)

A'COURT, ALAN

After joining Liverpool on his 18th birthday, Alan A'Court made his debut in a 3-2 win at Middlesborough but over the next two seasons drifted in and out of the side, only getting a chance when Scottish international Billy Liddell was selected at centre-forward. He eventually established himself in the side during the Reds' first season following relegation to the Second Division and was an important member of the side that struggled for promotion and which was eventually achieved in 1961-62. After representing the Football League and making seven appearances for England Under-23s, he made his dull international debut against Northern Ireland in 1957 and the following year appeared in the World Cup Finals in Sweden. With the emergence of Peter Thompson, he found himself squeezed out of the side and after scoring 63 goals in 382 games, he left to join Tranmere Rovers.

He made his debut at Stockport County, scoring Rovers' third goal in a 3-2 win. In both of his two seasons with the Prenton Park club, they finished fifth in Division Four and in February 1966, he netted his only hat-trick for the club in a 4-2 win at Bradford City. He had scored 11 goals in 54 League and Cup games for Rovers when he left to hold various coaching jobs at Norwich, Chester, Crewe and Stoke as well as in Zambia.

AGGREGATE SCORES

The club's highest aggregate scores have come in the Football League Cup. In 1991-92, a John Aldridge hat-trick helped Rovers beat Halifax Town 4-3 at The Shay, whilst two goals apiece from Aldridge and Steel at Prenton Park saw the club triumph by the same scoreline for an aggregate win of 8-6. In 1993-94, Pat Nevin netted a hat-trick in a 5-1 home win over Oxford United, whilst a Kenny Irons goal gave Rovers a 1-1 draw at the Manor Ground and an aggregate win of 6-2.

ALDRIDGE, JOHN

Liverpool-born John Aldridge had supported the Reds from the Kop in his youth and although Liverpool had been interested in him, he was allowed to join Newport County after a spell playing for South Liverpool. In March 1984, Oxford United paid Newport £78,000 for him. It was money well spent for Aldridge's goals helped them into the First Division. He had scored 90 goals in 141 games for the Manor Ground club when Liverpool paid £750,000 to bring him back home.

Over the next few seasons, Aldridge was to prove almost as prolific as Ian Rush, scoring 63 goals in 104 League and Cup games. Eventually the return of Rush was to restrict his appearances and in September 1989 he was transferred to Spanish club Real Sociedad for £1 million. Here he continued to clock up the goals in spite of the tight marking of the Spanish defences but, in the summer of 1991, he joined Tranmere Rovers for £250,000.

He scored both goals on his debut in a 2-0 win at Brighton and net-

John Aldridge, (Number 8) heads a goal against Blackburn Rovers during his days with Liverpool

ted nine in his first five games. He scored hat-tricks against Halifax Town (Away 4-3) Grimsby Town (Home 5-1) Derby County (Home 4-3) and Newcastle United in the League Cup (Home 6-6) to end the season with 40 goals and so equal Bunny Bell's record of 1933-34. Aldridge was the club's top scorer for six consecutive seasons and in 1992-93 he netted two more hat-tricks in the defeats of Wolves (Home 3-0) and League Cup opponents West Ham United (Home 5-2). Further hat-tricks followed in 1994-95 against Luton Town (Home 4-2) and West Bromwich Albion (Home 3-1) before he found the net four times in the 6-1 defeat of Barnsley.

In April 1996, he became the Prenton Park club's player-manager following the departure of John King and ended the campaign as the First Division's leading goalscorer. In 1996-97, his first full season as the club's player-manager, he again topped the club's scoring charts but decided after scoring 19 goals in 69 games for the Republic of Ireland to retire from international football just one goal short of equalling their scoring record. At the end of the 1997-98 season, after which he had scored 174 goals in 294 games for Rovers, he decided to hang up his boots as a first team player and concentrate fully on management.

ALLEN, RUSSELL

Birmingham-born Russell Allen was an apprentice with Arsenal before leaving Highbury to join West Bromwich Albion in May 1971. Unable to make the grade at the Hawthorns, he joined Tranmere Rovers in the summer of 1973 and made his first team debut in a 1-0 defeat at Charlton Athletic in October 1973 when he came on as a substitute for Eddie Loyden. He established himself as a first team regular the following season and in 1975-76 he helped the club win promotion from the Fourth Division.

In 1976-77 he was the club's leading scorer in the Third Division with 16 goals in 43 games but at the end of the following campaign after which he had taken his tally of goals for Rovers to 46 in 170 League and Cup games, he left Prenton Park to join Mansfield Town.

With the Stags he played in a more defensive midfield role and in three seasons with the Field Mill club, he scored 18 goals in 116 league games before leaving the first-class scene.

ANDERSON, DOUG

Outside-left Doug Anderson was born in Hong Kong but played his early football with Port Glasgow before joining Oldham Athletic. Unable to win a regular place in the Latics' side, he moved to Tranmere Rovers in the summer of 1984. He made his first team debut as a substitute for Mark Ferguson in a 3-2 League Cup defeat by Preston North End and played his first league game four days later as Crewe Alexandra were beaten 3-1.

An ever-present in 1985-86 when he scored 13 goals in 54 games, he gave Rovers three years good service, scoring 20 goals in 147 games before leaving to play for Plymouth Argyle. He later had loan spells with Cambridge United and Northampton Town before hanging up his boots.

ANDERSON, TED

Ted Anderson began his Football League career with Wolverhampton Wanderers after Major Frank Buckley signed him from Worksop Town. He couldn't win a regular place in the Molineux club's side and in December 1931, joined Torquay United. He made 61 league appearances for the Devon club before later playing for West Ham United and Chester City. Anderson joined Tranmere Rovers in the summer of 1937 and made his debut in a 5-0 home win over Carlisle United in September 1937. Noted for his long throw-ins, he went on to appear in 24 games that season as Rovers won the Third Division (North) Championship.

When league football resumed in 1946-47, Ted Anderson was the Rovers' captain and went on to appear in 79 games for the club before deciding to retire at the end of the 1947-48 season. After a spell as the 'A' team coach, he became the club's trainer.

ANGLO ITALIAN CUP

When Swindon Town won the Football League Cup in 1969, they were ineligible for the Fairs Cup because they were not a First Division side. Consequently they organised a match against the Italian League Cup winners, AS Roma, playing for the Anglo-Italian League Cup. The following year, the Anglo-Italian Cup was introduced for club sides from the two countries who had no involvement in Europe.

Tranmere first entered the competition when it was reintroduced in 1992-93. Their results were as follows:

Peterborough United (Away) 0-0	Wolves (Home) 2-1
AC Reggiana (Away) 0-0	US Cremonese (Home) 1-2
Pisa Sporting Club (Away) 1-0	Cosenza (Home) 2-1

In 1993-94, Rovers failed to get past the home group games, losing to:

Sunderland (Away) 0-2	Bolton Wanderers (Home) 1-2

In 1994-95 the club played four matches all against Italian opposition but failed to win one game:

Venezia (Home) 2-2	Atalanta (Away) 0-2
Ascoli (Home) 0-1	Lecce (Away) 0-3

APPEARANCES

The players with the highest number of appearances for Tranmere Rovers are as follows:

	League	FA Cup	F Lg Cup	Others	Total
Harold Bell	595	36	-	-	631
Ray Mathias	557 (10)	29 (1)	40	-	626 (11)
Steve Mungall	484 (34)	30 (1)	32 (3)	38 (2)	584 (40)
George Payne	439	25	3	-	467
Johnny Morrissey	373 (45)	27	33 (2)	30 (3)	463 (50)
Eric Nixon	352	19	34	34 (1)	439 (1)
Dave Higgins	349 (5)	20	28	32	429 (5)
Dickie Johnson	355	17	25	-	397
Steve Vickers	317 (1)	19	20 (1)	29	385 (2)
Ian Muir	286 (33)	17 (1)	22 (3)	26 (5)	351 (42)

ARNELL, ALAN

Alan Arnell joined Liverpool as an amateur in 1953 and scored on his debut in December 1954 as the Reds beat Blackpool 5-2 but it was not enough to save the Anfield club from relegation at the end of the season. The rest of Arnell's days with Liverpool were spent in the Second Division. His most prolific campaigns were 1955-56 and 1956-57 when he scored 23 goals in 37 outings including a hat-trick after pulling a muscle early in the game at Huddersfield Town in 1956. The big rangy centre-forward averaged a fraction short of a goal every two games for Liverpool but still couldn't convince his managers that he deserved a regular first team spot. In February 1961, Arnell, who had scored 35 goals in 75 games was sold to Tranmere Rovers in Bill Shankly's big Anfield clear-out.

After making his debut in a 4-1 home defeat at the hands of Walsall, Arnell played in all but one of the remaining 16 games of that season, scoring five goals. In 1961-62, he was the club's top scorer with 27 goals, a total which included hat-tricks against Middlesborough in the League Cup (Home 3-6) Chester (Home 4-1) and Colchester United (Home 5-2). He netted another hat-trick the following season in a 7-1 home win over Southport but in July 1963 he left Prenton Park having scored 38 goals in 71 games, to end his league career with Halifax Town.

ASSOCIATE MEMBERS CUP

The early rounds of this competition, announced by the Football League in December 1983 were run on knockout lines and played on a regional basis. In the first round, goals from Hilditch and Hutchinson gave Rovers a 2-0 win over Halifax Town, whilst the free-scoring Hilditch grabbed a hat-trick in the next round as Chester were beaten 4-1 at Prenton Park. In the Northern Area quarter-finals, Rovers played out a goalless draw against Crewe Alexandra before winning a penalty shoot-out 4-3. In the semi-finals Burnley were beaten 2-0 with Philpotts and Hilditch the Rovers scorers. In the Northern final, Tranmere visited Hull City but were well beaten 4-1 by the Tigers with Bobby Hutchinson scoring the Rovers goal.

ATKINSON, HAROLD

Bootle-born Harold Atkinson joined Tranmere Rovers from Liverpool County Combination side Carlton. He made his league debut in the opening game of the 1946-47 season, scoring Rovers' goal in a 4-1 home defeat by Rotherham United. He ended the season as the club's top scorer with 22 goals in 36 games including the first of five hat-tricks for Rovers in a 5-2 win over Lincoln City on Christmas Day. Atkinson, whose great timing in the air led to him scoring many of his goals with headers, topped the club's scoring charts in his first three seasons at Prenton Park.

His second hat-trick for the club came in the 4-2 FA Cup first round defeat of Goole Town in November 1951, just twelve months before he established a new FA Cup scoring record when he netted six goals in an 8-1 victory over Ashington. On New Year's Day 1954 he scored his fourth hat-trick for the club in a 3-2 win over Hartlepool United and his last in April 1955 in a 6-1 home defeat of Carlisle United. At the end of that season, Atkinson, who had scored 104 goals in 197 League and Cup games, left Prenton Park to join Chesterfield.

Unable to force his way into the first team at Saltergate, he played non-league football for Poole Town, Bangor City, Llandudno and New Brighton before returning to his trade as a joiner.

ATTENDANCE – AVERAGE

The average home league attendances of Tranmere Rovers over the last ten seasons have been as follows:

1988-89	5,331		1993-94	8,099
1989-90	7,449		1994-95	8,906
1990-91	6,740		1995-96	7,861
1991-92	8,845		1996-97	8,127
1992-93	8,071		1997-98	7,999

ATTENDANCE – HIGHEST

The record attendance at Prenton Park is 24,424 for the fourth round FA Cup game with Stoke City on 5 February 1972. The match ended in a 2-2 draw but Rovers lost the replay at the Victoria Ground 2-0.

The record attendance for a 'home' game is 61,036 for the FA Cup fourth round game against Liverpool on 27 January 1934 which was switched to Anfield and which the Reds won 3-1.

ATTENDANCE – LOWEST

The lowest attendance at Prenton Park is 937 for the visit of Halifax Town in an Associate Members Cup match on 20 February 1984. For the record, Rovers won 2-0 with goals from Hilditch and Hutchinson.

AWAY MATCHES

Tranmere Rovers' best away wins have all come in the Third Division (North). On 31 March 1928, Rovers beat Darlington 7-3, whilst they have scored six goals on their travels on two occasions, beating Rotherham United 6-4 on Christmas Day 1930 and Rochdale 6-3 on Boxing Day 1931.

Tranmere's worst defeat away from home is the 9-1 thrashing handed out to the Prenton Park club by Tottenham Hotspur in a third round FA Cup replay on 12 January 1953. The club also conceded nine goals in the Third Division match at Queen's Park Rangers on 3 December 1960, when they lost 9-2 at Loftus Road.

AWAY SEASONS

The club's highest number of away wins came in 1990-91 when they won 10 of their 23 matches when finishing fifth in Division Three. When Rovers finished bottom of the Second Division in 1938-39, they failed to win one single away game.

B

BAINBRIDGE, BILL

Gateshead-born inside-forward Bill Bainbridge played his early football with Ashington before joining Manchester United. After failing to make the grade at Old Trafford, he had a short spell with Bury before signing for Tranmere Rovers in November 1948. He made his debut in a 2-1 home win over Carlisle United and went on to score seven goals in 26 games in that campaign. In 1949-50, Bainbridge, who was one of only two ever-presents, was the club's top scorer with 19 goals as Rovers finished fifth in the Third Division (North). The following season he repeated the feat and included in his total of 19 goals was a sequence where he scored eight goals in seven consecutive games.

Possessing a powerful shot, the all-action forward went on to score 68 goals in 182 League and Cup games before leaving the club in 1953 to play non-league football for Ellesmere Port Town.

BARTON, TEDDY

Teddy Barton began his career with Everton but after being unable to force his way into the Goodison Park club's first team, he moved across the Mersey to join Tranmere Rovers. Though he made his league debut in a 3-2 home win over Bradford Park Avenue in February 1926, it was 1928-29 before he established himself as a first team regular at Prenton Park. In fact, he played in just seven games during his first three seasons with the club and in 1926-27 did not appear at all!

The tough-tackling right-half was a virtual ever-present for six seasons and though he only scored five goals for the club, the first in a 4-1 defeat at Hartlepool United in February 1929, he created a great number for players such as Billy Charlton, Jack Kennedy, Ernie Dixon and

Bunny Bell. Barton had played in 257 games for the club when he hung up his boots at the end of the 1934-35 season.

BEAMISH, KEN

Much-travelled striker Ken Beamish began his league career with Tranmere Rovers and made his debut in a goalless draw at Chester-field in April 1966. It was his only appearance that season and in 1966-67 when the club won promotion he again made just one ap-pearance. It was the latter end of the 1967-68 season when he estab-lished himself as a first team regular in the Rovers' side. The following season he was the club's joint-top scorer with George Yardley, his total of 14 goals including a hat-trick in a 6-2 home win over Oldham Athletic. He was the club's top scorer in 1970-71, net-ting hat-tricks against Crewe Alexandra (Home 4-0) and Rotherham United (Home 5-0). After topping the club's scoring charts again in 1971-72, he left Prenton Park to join Brighton and Hove Albion as they made their final push for promotion from Division Three. His Second Division career ended after just one season when Brighton were relegated and after one more season with the Seagulls he joined Blackburn Rovers for £30,000.

In his first season at Ewood Park he helped win the Third Division Championship and was second highest scorer. He found goals more difficult to come by in the higher grade of football and after scoring 28 goals in 98 games, he was allowed to join Port Vale for £10,000. After scoring 29 league goals for the Valiants he moved to Bury and main-tained his scoring record with 20 goals in 49 games.

In November 1979, he returned to Tranmere to play out the remain-der of his career. He was the club's top scorer in 1979-80 with 11 goals, a total which included his fourth hat-trick for the club in a 4-0 win over Bradford City., He had scored 81 goals in 278 games in his two spells with the club when he moved to Swindon Town in a coaching capacity. In March 1983, he was appointed manager of the County Ground club before returning to Ewood Park as Blackburn's Commercial Manager.

BELL, 'BUNNY'

Robert 'Bunny' Bell was the first player to score a triple hat-trick in

English league football when he scored nine of Tranmere Rovers' goals in the 13-4 win over Oldham Athletic on Boxing Day 1935 and he missed a penalty!

Born in Birkenhead, he joined Rovers from local club Carlton and made his debut in a 3-2 FA Cup defeat at Gateshead in December 1930 while still working as a shipping clerk. It was his only appearance that season but in 1931-32 he scored 12 goals in 11 games including hat-tricks in the wins over Darlington (Home 3-1) and Walsall (Home 4-1). In 1932-33 he was the club's joint-top scorer with 17 goals in 34 games but in 1933-34 he established a new club record with 40 League and Cup goals in 38 appearances. His total included four goals in the defeats of Barnsley (Home 5-2) and Newark Town in the FA Cup (Home 7-0) and hat-tricks against Chester (Home 6-1) Crewe Alexandra (Home 5-1) York City (Home 3-0) and Halifax Town (Home 3-2). Though injuries forced him to miss much of the following season, he was back to his best in 1935-36, scoring 38 goals in 33 games to top the club's scoring charts. His total included four goals in a 6-0 win over Accrington Stanley and hat-tricks against Stockport County (Home 4-1) and Scunthorpe United (Home 6-2) and of course his nine goals against Oldham Athletic, of which he scored five in the first-half and four in the second. Bell's record though was broken four months later when Luton's Joe Payne scored 10 goals in the club's 12-0 win over Bristol Rovers.

In March 1936, Everton signed Bunny Bell, primarily as cover for Tommy Lawton, in exchange for Archie Clark. Though he only played in two games for the Blues that season, he scored three goals to become the only player to average more than a goal per game in both Division One and Three in the same season! He went on to score nine goals in 14 games for the Goodison Park club before hanging up his boots.

BELL, HAROLD

The club's longest-serving player, Harold Bell joined Tranmere Rovers just before the outbreak of the Second World War with a reputation at schoolboy level for being a prolific goalscorer. Despite scoring a hat-trick on his debut for the club in a 6-4 win over Bradford Park Avenue in April 1941, the 16-year-old Bell was converted to centre-half and later to full-back. Having appeared in around 200 games for the club during the war years, he made his league debut in a 4-1 home defeat at the hands of Rotherham United on the opening day of the 1946-47 season.

Bell was ever-present for the first nine seasons of league football after the hostilities, appearing in 401 consecutive games between 1946 and 1955, plus another 26 in the FA Cup.

One of the club's most respected captains, he went on to appear in 631 League and Cup games before ending his career with Holyhead Town.

BELMONT F.C.

Belmont FC were the forerunners of the present Tranmere Rovers and were formed in 1884 by two groups of cricketers, Belmont CC and Lyndhurst Wanderers. The club's first president was James Hannay McGaul JP and most of the players, members of the local Wesleyan Chapel.

The club played their first game on 15 November 1884, beating Brunswick Rovers 4-0. During that 1884-85 season, Belmont played 15 friendly matches, losing only one. On 16 September 1885, just before the start of their second season, the club changed their name to Tranmere Rovers.

BEST STARTS

Tranmere Rovers were unbeaten for the first nine games of seasons 1923-24 and 1935-36. In 1923-24 the club won three and drew six of their matches before losing 2-1 at home to New Brighton on 13 October 1923. In 1935-36, the club won six and drew three of their matches before going down for the first time at Wrexham on 12 October 1935 by 4-0.

BLACKBURN, ERNIE

After playing league football for Aston Villa and Bradford City, Ernie Blackburn joined Accrington Stanley as trainer in the summer of 1924, becoming secretary-manager a few months later. At Accrington he had to work under the burden of financial problems and though he had charge of the day-to-day running of the club, the directors picked the team.

In January 1932 he was appointed as Wrexham's manager and in his first season with the Welsh club almost took them to promotion as runners-up to Hull City. He stayed at Wrexham until January 1937 when he was offered the manager's job at Boothferry Park. He helped reduce the Yorkshire club's debts but after keeping the club going through the war years, Blackburn was surprisingly not retained at the end of the hostilities and became the first manager to lose his job after the war.

In September 1946 he was appointed as manager of Tranmere Rovers and over the next few years brought some fine players to Prenton Park, notably Harry Eastham and Cyril Done. Blackburn's sides were both successful and entertaining but in 1955 he relinquished team duties to concentrate on administration.

BOXING DAY

In the 1930s, there was something special about Tranmere Rovers' games played on Boxing Day. In addition to the league record 13-4 score in their club record win against Oldham Athletic in 1935, they also suffered a 9-3 defeat in 1938 at the hands of Manchester City, during their first season in Division Two. On 25 December 1931, Tranmere had beaten Rochdale 9-1 and the following day won 6-3 at Spotland in a Third Division (North) game.

BRAMHALL, JOHN

Centre-half John Bramhall played his early football with Stockton Heath before Tranmere Rovers brought him to Prenton Park in the summer of 1976. His first game for the club came in September 1976 as Rovers were beaten 3-1 at home by Brighton and Hove Albion. However, it was 1978-79 before he won a regular place in the heart of the Tranmere defence, though at the end of the season, the club were relegated to the Fourth Division. In fact, two seasons later, Rovers had to apply for re-election to the League after finishing 21st. Bramhall had scored eight goals in 193 first team outings when in March 1982 he signed for Bury.

Bramhall helped the Shakers win promotion from the Fourth Division in 1984-85 but after a loan spell at Chester, the popular defender, who had scored 17 goals in 167 games joined local rivals Rochdale.

He continued to score goals from his position at the heart of the Spotland club's defence, netting 13 in 86 games. He later played for Halifax Town before ending his league career with Scunthorpe United.

BRANNAN, GED

Equally at home in central midfield or in either of the full-back spots, Ged Brannan made his Rovers' debut in October 1990 when he came on as a substitute for Johnny Morrissey in a 6-2 home win over Mansfield Town. He went on to appear in 27 first team games that season and played left-back in the play-off final win over Bolton Wanderers at Wembley that took Rovers into the Second Division.

Ged Brannan, a great servant of the Prenton Park Club

Over the next six seasons, Brannan was a virtual ever-present with his best season in terms of goals scored, being 1993-94 when he found the net 11 times in 58 games.

He went on to score 25 goals in 303 League and Cup games before leaving Prenton Park in March 1997 and joining Manchester City for £750,000. His contract had been due to expire at the end of the season and with Rovers eager to act as quickly as possible because of the Bosman ruling, he left for a sum which was thought to be well below his current valuation.

He was an ever-present in the City side until New Year 1998 but then Frank Clark changed the system and he lost his place. Despite suffering a hairline leg fracture he went on to appear in 46 games before leaving Maine Road to join Motherwell.

BRIGGS, ARTHUR

Goalkeeper Arthur Briggs joined Tranmere Rovers from Hull City and made his debut in October 1924 in a 1-0 home defeat by Walsall. He went on to appear in 28 league games in a season in which Rovers finished next to the bottom of the Third Division (North) and had to apply for re-election. Despite conceding 15 goals in the games against Grimsby Town (Away 0-8) and Nelson (Away 0-7), Briggs was ever-present in 1925-26 and again two seasons later when Rovers ended the campaign in fifth place, their highest league position at that time.

He went on to play in 246 League and Cup games for the Prenton Park club, making his last appearance in a 5-2 home win over Halifax Town in December 1932. He joined Swindon Town and in three seasons at the County Ground made 60 appearances, helping the club finish eighth in the Third Division (South) in 1933-34.

BROTHERS

There have been a number of instances of brothers playing for Tranmere Rovers. Ray and Keith Williams played for Rovers during the 1950s. Ray who scored 16 goals in 214 games for the Prenton Park club was nearing the end of his career when younger brother Keith made it into Rovers' first team. A former Everton junior, he scored on his Tranmere debut and ended his first season with the club as the leading scorer – his total of 30 goals included three hat-tricks. He went on to score 97 goals in 173 games before joining Plymouth Argyle.

Keith and Ray Davies also played for Rovers during the 1950s, though when Keith played his only game for the club in a 1-0 defeat at home to Bradford City, Ray, who made 136 first team appearances, was missing.

In the summer of 1961, Rovers signed a pair of identical twins in David and Peter Jackson. More information on the players can be found under the heading of 'Twins', though they did play together in the same Tranmere team on 24 occasions.

Another pair of brothers to have played for Rovers were Stan and Trevor Storton who had similar playing records for the Prenton Park club. Trevor who was 10 years younger than Stan eventually left Rovers to play for Liverpool.

BURGESS, DAVE

After being rejected by Everton, full-back Dave Burgess joined Tranmere Rovers as a part-timer in the summer of 1981 and made his first team debut in a 2-0 home defeat at the hands of York City on the opening day of the 1981-82 season. During the course of that campaign, in which he was the club's only ever-present, he scored his only goal for Tranmere in a 3-1 home win over Blackpool. Burgess, who was also ever-present in 1982-83, appeared in 159 consecutive games from his debut.

Though his performances attracted the attention of a host of top clubs, it was to Grimsby Town that he left in August 1986 after having played in 260 games for Rovers.

He was a regular in the Mariners' side for two seasons before leaving Blundell Park in July 1988 to join Blackpool. Burgess appeared in exactly 100 games for the Seasiders before hanging up his boots.

C

CAMPBELL, JOHNNY

Wing-half Johnny Campbell joined Rovers in 1914 but like so many other players of his generation, he found his career interrupted by the First World War. Despite having a bullet embedded in his skull during the hostilities, Campbell returned to Prenton Park for the 1919-20 season. After impressing in the club's Central League side, he won a place in the Tranmere side for the club's first-ever league game when they beat Crewe Alexandra 4-1. After that he was a regular member of the club's first team for the next six seasons, though he missed the entire 1926-27 season through injury. He continued to play for the club until the end of the 1929-30 season, making the last of his 204 appearances in which he scored 11 goals in an 8-0 defeat at Lincoln City in April 1930!

CAPACITY

The total capacity of Prenton Park in 1998-99 was 16,789.

CARR, JACK

The most famous of five footballing brothers, Jack Carr was playing for South Bank East End when Sunderland rejected him as being too small. In 1910, South Bank reached the FA Amateur Cup Final and though they lost to Royal Marine Light Infantry, he had done enough to impress Middlesbrough who signed him there and then.

He scored twice on his debut against Nottingham Forest and local folklore has it that the 9 stone Carr had his jersey and shorts 'tightened' with safety pins for the big occasion. In the first post-war season he was capped by England against Ireland and won his second cap against Wales in 1923. A key figure in 'Boro's two Second Division title-winning seasons of the 1920s, he went on to score 81 goals in 449 games before joining Blackpool. After helping the Seasiders win promotion to the First Division, he became player-coach of Hartlepool United before managing them from 1932 to 1935.

In July 1935 he was appointed as manager of Tranmere Rovers from over 60 applicants for the post. Having led the Third Division (North) for much of the following season, the club slipped up over the last few games to end the campaign in third place. During the season the club beat Oldham Athletic 13-4 to record their biggest-ever league victory. The 1936-37 season saw Rovers struggle in the lower reaches of the Third Division (North) and in November 1936 he left the club, later managing Darlington.

CARTMAN, BERT

Outside-left Bert Cartman began his Football League career with Manchester United but after making just three league appearances in the 1922-23 season, he left Old Trafford to join Tranmere Rovers.

He played his first game for the Prenton Park club in a 2-1 home win over Grimsby Town on the opening day of the 1923-24 season and went on to appear in all but one of the club's league games that season. He repeated the feat in 1924-25 and was a first team regular for seven seasons. A good crosser of the ball, he created a number of chances for colleagues Stan Sayer and Dixie Dean, whilst his best season in terms of goals scored was 1928-29 when he netted eight times in 29 games. Cartman left Prenton Park in the summer of 1930, having scored 33 goals in 234 League and Cup games to play non-league football for Chorley.

CENTRAL LEAGUE

The Central League was formed in 1911 by the Northern and Midland giants of the Football League as a reserve team league. The first-ever winners were not, however giants, but Lincoln City – who won it with 48 points out of a possible 64 and then immediately withdrew from the League, never to return.

Rovers first entered the Central League in 1919-20 replacing Leeds City who had been disbanded by the Football Association following an inquiry about illegal payments and inducements to players. As part of their conditions on gaining acceptance to the Central League, Rovers had to take over Leeds' record of six points from seven games but still managed to finish fourth. In 1920-21, Rovers finished seventh, this earning them a place in the Third Division (North) the following season.

On their return to the Central League, Rovers won the Second Division Championship in 1993-94, finishing 12 points clear of runners-up West Bromwich Albion. The club lost their First Division status in 1997-98 when they finished 12th out of the 13 clubs.

CENTURIES

There are four instances of individual players who have scored 100 or more league goals for Tranmere Rovers. Ian Muir is the greatest goalscorer with 142 strikes in his Prenton Park career (1985-1994). Other centurions are John Aldridge (133) Bunny Bell (102) and Barry Dyson (100).

Harold Bell holds the record for the most consecutive league appearances – 401. Other players to have made over 100 consecutive league appearances during their Tranmere careers are: Ray Mathias (200); Ray Mathias (137 in a second spell); Dave Burgess (135); Fred Urmson (134); Ian Muir (133); Clive Evans (131); Jim Cumbes (126); Steve Vickers (125); Dickie Johnson (121); Steve Mungall (121); Tom Stuart (113); and Eric Nixon (108).

CHAMPIONSHIPS

Tranmere Rovers have won a divisional championship of the Football League on just one occasion and that was in 1937-38 when they were champions of the Third Division (North).

The club's leading scorer was Pongo Waring with 22 goals, whilst the only other Rovers' player to get into double figures was Billy Eden with 12 goals. The club clinched the Championship with five points from their last three games of the season – Hull City (Away 1-0) Lincoln City (Away 1-0) and runners-up Doncaster Rovers (Away 1-1) – if Rovers had lost this last game, the title would have gone to the Belle Vue club!

CHARLTON, BILLY

Inside-forward Billy Charlton joined Tranmere Rovers from Cardiff City in 1926, having failed to make the grade with the Welsh club. He made his debut for Rovers at Lincoln City on 13 March 1926, scoring twice in a 3-1 win. The following season he played in 22 games scoring 11 goals but it was 1927-28 when he really came to the fore, ending the season as the club's joint-top scorer with Pongo Waring with 24 goals in 41 games. His total included his first hat-trick for the club in a 5-3 home win over Ashington. His second hat-trick came twelve months later as Rochdale were beaten 5-1 at Prenton Park.

In 1929-30, his last season with the club, he was Rovers' leading scorer with 20 goals in 43 games as they finished the campaign in 12th place in the Third Division (North).

One of the club's most prolific goalscorers, he had found the net 74 times in 137 League and Cup games before surprisingly being allowed to leave Prenton Park and join Workington.

CHESHIRE COUNTY LEAGUE

The club's reserve side were members of the Cheshire County League from its inaugural season of 1919-20 (when they withdrew after just six games in order to facilitate their membership of the Central League) until 1970 when it was disbanded. Though Rovers scored 163 goals in 1926-27, their best season was 1937-38 when they won the Championship with the following record:

P.	W.	D.	L.	F.	A.	Pts
42	30	6	6	148	45	66

CLARK, ARCHIE

Centre-half Archie Clark began his league career with Luton Town where after a series of impressive performances, Everton were alerted and signed him in May 1931. In his first season at Goodison Park, he played in 39 league games and scored one of the goals in Everton's 9-2 home win over Leicester City. That season the Blues won the League Championship, but for Clark it was virtually the end of his first team career at Goodison Park. He stayed with Everton until March 1936 but only made two more league appearances for the club.

On joining Tranmere Rovers, Clark went straight into the side and made his debut later that month in a 2-1 defeat at Stockport County. He was an important member of the Tranmere side for the next three seasons and in 1937-38 helped the club win the Third Division (North) Championship. During that campaign he scored his only goal for the club in a 2-1 home win over Port Vale. He had made 108 appearances for the Prenton Park club when he left to end his career with Gillingham.

CLARKE, COLIN

The family of much-travelled striker Colin Clarke moved from Newry to Ipswich when he was 12 and so consequently he joined the Portman Road club as an apprentice. He failed to make the grade with Ipswich and joined Peterborough United on a free transfer. After playing in 82 league games for the London Road club, he joined Tranmere Rovers after a loan spell at Gillingham.

He made his debut in a 1-0 defeat against his former club on the opening day of the 1984-85 season with Peterborough's winner coming against the run of play. Though this was his only season with the Prenton Park club, he formed a prolific goalscoring partnership with John Clayton and scored 29 goals in 53 games including a hat-trick in a 7-0 first round FA Cup win over Bangor City.

In the summer of 1985 he signed for Third Division Bournemouth where his goalscoring feats won him the first of 38 international caps for Northern Ireland and the attention of a number of top foreign clubs, including Torino of Italy. His performances for Northern Ireland in the 1986 World Cup led to Southampton paying £400,000 for his services.

Clarke made immediate history by becoming the first Southampton player to score a hat-trick on his debut in a 5-1 win over Queen's Park Rangers and followed this with another three goals in a 4-1 home win over Newcastle United in October 1986. After ending the season as the club's leading scorer, he began to suffer from injuries and had a loan spell back at Bournemouth before joining Queen's Park Rangers. One season later he signed for Portsmouth for a club record fee of £415,000 and scored 27 goals in 107 first team appearances before retiring from the game.

CLAYTON, JOHN

A Scottish Schoolboy international, he joined Derby County as an apprentice but then left the Football League to join the Hong Kong side Bulova in 1982-83. Returning to this country, he played in 33 league games for Chesterfield before joining Tranmere Rovers in the summer of 1984.

He made his debut for the Prenton Park club in a 1-0 defeat at Peterborough United on the opening day of the 1984-85 season before scoring on his home debut in a 3-2 League Cup defeat by Preston North End. That season, Clayton made his mark as the country's leading marksman with 36 goals including a hat-trick in a 3-0 home win over Stockport County and eight 'doubles'. He played in the opening three games of the 1985-86 season, netting a hat-trick in a 6-2 home win over Cambridge United and one on his final appearance for the club in a 2-2 draw at Preston North End.

He had scored 40 goals in 55 games when he left Rovers to join Plymouth Argyle as a replacement for Tommy Tynan. However, when Tynan rejoined the Devon club, the two formed a good forward partnership. Clayton went on to score 22 goals in 77 games before leaving Home Park after three years to join Dutch Division One club, Fortuna Sittard for £65,000.

CLEAN SHEET

This is the colloquial expression to describe a goalkeeper's performance when he does not concede a goal. Eric Nixon in 1988-89 had 20 clean sheets from 45 league appearances, plus another five in Cup competitions. The next best performance is by Frankie Lane who kept 19 clean sheets in 44 appearances in 1970-71.

COLOURS

Belmont FC wore blue shirts and white knickers as did the early Rovers' sides but in 1889, the club adopted an unusual combination of maroon and orange halved shirts and navy blue knickers! It was around 1904 when Rovers reverted to the blue and white colours which have in some way remained until today. Dave Russell's side of 1962-63 played in an all-white strip with blue edging and, though blue shirts were later adopted, Rovers returned to an all-white strip with blue socks.

The club's present colours are white shirts and blue shorts, whilst the club's change colours are orange, green and white.

CONSECUTIVE HOME GAMES

Tranmere have played an extraordinary intense sequence of five home games in succession on six occasions and three times won all five games. They were:

1931-32

28 November	West Stanley	FA Cup Rd 1	Won 3-0
5 December	Halifax Town	Div 3 (N)	Won 5-2
12 December	Bristol Rovers	FA Cup Rd 2	Won 2-0
19 December	Gateshead	Div 3 (N)	Won 4-3
25 December	Rochdale	Div 3 (N)	Won 9-1

1935-36

23 November	Chester	Div 3 (N)	Won 3-1
30 November	Carlisle United	FA Cup Rd 1	Won 3-0
7 December	Rochdale	Div 3 (N)	Won 5-2
14 December	Scunthorpe United	FA Cup Rd 2	Won 6-2
21 December	Barrow	Div 3 (N)	Won 1-0

1937-38

20 November	Barrow	Div 3 (N)	Won 3-0
27 November	Carlisle United	FA Cup Rd 1	Won 2-1
4 December	Hartlepool United	Div 3 (N)	Won 4-0
11 December	Hartlepool United	FA Cup Rd 2	Won 3-1
18 December	Hull City	Div 3 (N)	Won 3-1

CONSECUTIVE SCORING – LONGEST SEQUENCE

Jack Kennedy holds the club record for consecutive scoring when he was on target in eight consecutive league games. He netted a hat-trick in a 7-3 home win over Rochdale in the first of the sequence on 20 September 1930 and ended the run with two goals in a 4-3 defeat at Wigan Borough on 8 November 1930.

Ernie Dixon has also scored in eight consecutive games but these included two FA Cup ties. His first came in the 2-2 draw with Chester at Prenton Park on 7 November 1931 and ended with the fourth goal in the 6-3 win at Rochdale on Boxing Day 1931.

COOKE, BERT

Bert Cooke joined the club's office staff in 1909 and three years later was appointed secretary-manager. He was instrumental in bringing league football to Prenton Park in 1921 and signing some fine players including Dixie Dean, Ellis Rimmer and Pongo Waring.

On 30 April 1935, Cooke was suddenly sacked following board-room wrangles over alleged illegal payments to both directors and players. Though the Tranmere board were suspended, Cooke was the scapegoat and a FA Commission banned him.

It was a sad end to a fine career which saw Rovers finish fourth in the Third Division (North) in seasons 1930-31 and 1931-32.

COPPELL, STEVE

Born in Croxteth, University graduate Steve Coppell was spotted by Rovers' scout Eddie Edwards and after playing in a Liverpool Senior Cup match against Liverpool was given his league debut in a 1-0 home defeat by Aldershot in January 1974. He went on to score 11 goals in 45 games before Bill Shankly who was acting as a consultant to the Wirral club recommended him to Tommy Docherty the manager of Manchester United after his own club had failed to show any interest.

Coppell joined the Old Trafford club for £60,000 in February 1975. He went on to score 70 goals in 395 games and pick up 42 England caps. A fast winger with the ability to cut inside as well as race down the flanks, he appeared in three FA Cup Finals, picking up a winners'

Steve Coppell who, after leaving Prenton Park, went on to make 42 appearances for England.

medal in 1977. He won his first cap against Italy in November 1977 and was a member of the 1982 World Cup squad that went to Spain. He played his last match for England in 1983 against Greece. By then a persistent knee injury was interrupting his appearances. He finally gave up the fight against injury in the summer of 1983 and accepted the offer of a job as manager of Crystal Palace. At 28 he was the youngest manager in the Football League but despite leading the Eagles to the 1990 FA Cup Final, he resigned his post during the summer of 1993 following Palace's relegation. He then became the Selhurst Park club's director of football before managing Manchester City for a short spell in 1996. He returned to Palace and took over the reins following Terry Venables' departure in 1998-99.

COYNE, DANNY

A product of the club's impressive youth policy, he made his Tranmere debut in a 1-1 draw at Peterborough United in May 1993, though over the next three seasons the Prestatyn-born 'keeper only made 13 appearances. Having replaced Eric Nixon towards the end of the 1994-95 season, Coyne kept his place throughout the following season, becoming an ever-present as the side finished 13th in the First Division.

His bravery and safe handling brought the Premier League scouts flocking to Prenton Park and he made his full international debut for Wales when he played against Switzerland.

On New Year's Day 1997 he was involved in an accidental clash in the match at West Bromwich Albion and was left with badly-torn neck ligaments. Since then he has been plagued by a series of persistent injuries but will be looking to add to his 110 appearances for the club.

CRICKETERS

The only Tranmere Rovers player who was a cricketer of any real note was goalkeeper Jim Cumbes. He played first-class cricket for four counties, Surrey, Lancashire, Worcestershire and Warwickshire. He took 379 wickets in a career that spanned 20 years from 1963 to 1983, winning County Championship and Gillette Cup winners' medals with Worcestershire.

CRISIS

In the summer of 1900, a group of Rovers' players went to see the club's President James Hannay McGaul to ask if he would consider the club moving to Bedford Park which was now vacant following the demise of Rock Ferry. McGaul would not listen and was adamant that the club stay at Prenton Park. This led to almost all the players leaving Tranmere to join Birkenhead, a newly formed club who were to be based at Bedford Park. After just one season, the Birkenhead club were forced to leave Bedford Park and gradually over the next few years, the players who had left Rovers began to drift back.

The club encountered another crisis during the 1982-83 season when a 'Save the Rovers' fund was formed following a failed bid by Billy McAteer, an American-based tycoon. A host of top clubs came to Prenton Park to play friendlies but it was Wirral Borough Council who eventually saved the club with a £200,000 loan.

In January 1987, American Chairman Bruce Osterman failed in his bid to sell off Prenton Park for supermarket development and threatened to wind up the club. Director George Higham and secretary Norman Wilson applied to the High Court for an Administration Order until the 1986 Insolvency Act. Stripped of his power, Osterman eventually sold his majority shareholding to Peter Johnson who became the club's new owner.

CROSSLEY, PAUL

Rochdale-born winger Paul Crossley began his league career with his home-town club before moving to Preston North End in November 1966. Unable to win a regular place in the Deepdale club's side, he was loaned out to Southport before Tranmere Rovers paid £5,000 to take him to Prenton Park in the summer of 1969.

He made his debut in a 3-2 home win over Bury in September 1969, a match in which George Yardley netted a hat-trick for Rovers. Over the next five seasons, Crossley became noted for his fine pin-point crosses which Eddie Loyden amongst others put away in great style. However, Crossley too knew where the net was and in season's 1973-74 and 1974-75, was the club's top scorer. In 1975 he spent the summer playing for Seattle Sounders in the NASL but after arriving back late for the start of the new season, found he had lost his place.

Crossley, who had scored 45 goals in 229 games, joined Chester in exchange for John James plus a cash adjustment. He enjoyed three good seasons at Sealand Road, netting 26 times in 99 league outings.

CROWD TROUBLE

However unwelcome, crowd disturbances are far from being a modern phenomenon at Football League matches.

When Rovers entertained Heywood United in a Lancashire Combination match during Christmas 1912, the referee was attacked by fans who invaded the Prenton Park playing area. This resulted in the ground being shut for two weeks as a punishment. Though thankfully there has been nothing as serious as that since, there have been a number of incidents where missiles have been thrown. Perhaps the worst of these was in the FA Cup second round tie against Hull City in 1984.

On a lighter note, when Rovers lost 5-0 at home to Bournemouth on 28 September 1979, 72-year-old Tranmere fanatic Charlie Lindsay took it upon himself to smack the Cherries' 'keeper Kenny Allen across the backside with his walking stick!

CUMBES, JIM

Jim Cumbes, goalkeeper and first-class cricketer.

After playing his early football for Runcorn, goalkeeper Jim Cumbes turned professional with Tranmere Rovers, helping them win promotion to the Third Division in his first season. He had made his debut in a goalless draw at home to Chester on the opening day of the 1966-67 season, a campaign in which he kept 17 clean sheets. Cumbes was also ever-present in his first two seasons at Prenton Park and went on to play in 126 consecutive league games. After playing in 156 League and Cup games, the last of which was a 3-0 win over Stockport County on the opening day of the 1969-70 season, he joined West Bromwich Albion for £33,350. He spent two years at the Hawthorns, playing in 64 league games before signing for Aston Villa for £36,000. In his first season with the Villans he won a Third Division Championship medal. In 1974-75, he played in all but four of Villa's games as they won promotion to the top flight and collected a winners' tankard when Villa won the League Cup. He left Villa in March 1974 to join his old boss Vic Crowe at Portland Timbers before returning to this country to play non-league football with Runcorn, Southport, Worcester City and Kidderminster Harriers.

A more than useful fast bowler, he played first-class cricket for Surrey, Lancashire, Worcestershire and Warwickshire.

D

DEAN, DIXIE

Arguably the greatest goalscorer that the game has ever known, Dixie Dean carved a very special niche for himself in Merseyside sporting folklore.

He once scored 18 goals in a day, six goals each in three games. In the morning he played in a Birkenhead Schoolboys trial, in the afternoon he turned out for Laird Street School and in the evening he played for Moreton Bible Class.

He made his league debut for Tranmere Rovers in a 5-1 defeat at Rotherham County in January 1924. But it was during the following campaign that he gave notice that he was about to become a major force in the game when he top-scored with 27 goals in 27 league games at the age of 17. His total included three hat-tricks against Hartlepool United (Home 4-3) Barrow (Home 4-1) and Rochdale (Home 3-1), though Rovers finished 21st in the Third Division (North) and had to apply for re-election.

Everton were one of the first clubs to spot his talents and Tom McIntosh the club secretary was sent over the water to sign the young player. Dean was delighted when he arrived home to be told by his mother that an Everton official had been wanting to talk to him. He was so excited that he ran the three miles to the Woodside Hotel to meet McIntosh and signed for the Blues there and then. Five days later on 21 March 1925, he made his debut in a 3-1 defeat against Arsenal at Highbury. A week later, he made his homed debut and scored a goal in Everton's 2-0 win over Aston Villa. In his first full season with the club he scored 32 goals in 38 games including four hat-tricks.

He came very close to death in a motor-cycle crash which left him unconscious for 36 hours with a broken jawbone and a fractured skull. His remarkable constitution and iron will pulled him through and within 15 weeks of the accident he was back and scoring in the Blues' first team.

The pinnacle of his career was reached in 1927-28 when he scored 60 goals in 39 league games, including all five in a 5-2 home win over Manchester United and four in a 5-3 win at Burnley as well as five hat-tricks as Everton won the League Championship.

In 1938 he severed his ties with the Goodison club when he joined Notts County. He had worn the blue shirt on 431 occasions and scored 377 goals. He had been capped 16 times by his country and won every honour the game could bestow on him. After playing in just nine games for Notts County, he moved on to Irish club Sligo but the Second World War interrupted and he retired from the game to run the Dublin Packet pub in Chester.

Sadly in 1976 his right leg was amputated after a long illness. Four years later at Goodison Park just a minute before the final whistle of the Merseyside derby, he collapsed and died.

DEBUTS

Only two players have scored hat-tricks for the club on their Football League debuts. The first was Jack Flanagan who scored all three goals in a 3-1 defeat of Wigan Borough on 6 November 1927. He went on to score 26 goals that season and top the club's scoring charts. The second Rovers' player to score a hat-trick on his debut was Billy Woodward in a 5-0 home win over Southport on the opening day of the 1933-34 season. The two players also have another connection in that they both joined the Prenton Park club from Manchester United.

DEFEATS – FEWEST

During the 1988-89 season, Tranmere Rovers went through the full

46-match programme and only suffered eight defeats as they won promotion, finishing runners-up to Rotherham United in the Fourth Division Championship.

DEFEATS – MOST

Tranmere's total of 31 defeats during the 1938-39 season is the worst in the club's history. Not surprisingly, Rovers finished bottom of the Second Division and were relegated.

DEFEATS – WORST

Tranmere Rovers' worst home defeat in the Football League occurred on Boxing Day 1938 when Manchester City beat them 9-3 in front of a Prenton Park crowd of 13,378. The club's worst defeat away from home in the league came at Queen's Park Rangers on 3 December 1960 when the Loftus Road club won 9-2. The London club also beat Rovers 6-0 in the League Cup in September 1969, a scoreline repeated by West Ham United in September 1974. Rovers have also conceded nine goals in the FA Cup when Spurs beat them 9-1 at White Hart Lane in a third round replay in January 1953 after the first match had been drawn 1-1.

DEFENSIVE RECORD

Tranmere Rovers' best defensive record was established in 1937-38 and helped the club win the Third Division (North) Championship. They conceded just 41 goals in that campaign and were beaten in only nine matches.

The club's worst defensive record was in 1960-61 when they let in 115 goals to finish 21st in the Third Division and were relegated to the league's basement for the first time in their history.

DERBIES

Though Tranmere Rovers have never met Everton or Liverpool in the Football League, they have played both clubs in the two major cup competitions.

In 1933-34, Rovers were drawn at home to Liverpool in the fourth round of the FA Cup but switched the tie to Anfield to enable a club record crowd of 60,036 to see the game. Bill Meacock scored for Rovers in a 3-1 defeat. In 1960-61, a Frank Wignall hat-trick helped Everton to a 4-0 win at Prenton Park in a fourth round League Cup tie. In 1967-68, Rovers reached the fifth round of the FA Cup only to lose 2-0 to Everton at Goodison Park. The following season Rovers went down 4-0 away from home to Everton in a League Cup second round tie. In 1979-80, Rovers met Liverpool at the same stage of the League Cup competition but, after a goalless draw at Prenton Park, the Reds ran out winners 4-0 in the replay at Anfield.

DIXON, ERNIE

Ernie Dixon joined Tranmere Rovers from Nelson in the summer of 1930 after a number of impressive performances against the Prenton Park club in meetings between the two clubs in the Third Division (North). He made his debut in the opening game of the 1930-31 season as Rovers won 3-1 at Barrow. He ended the campaign with 32 goals in 43 games including a hat-trick in an 8-0 home win over Accrington Stanley. He also scored twice against his former club at Prenton Park in a 7-1 win and another at Nelson where Rovers completed the 'double' by winning 4-0. Forming a prolific goalscoring partnership with Jack Kennedy, Ernie Dixon was the club's top scorer in 1931-32 with 22 goals including a spell of 10 goals in eight consecutive matches. The following season he suffered from a loss of form and a series of niggling injuries and after taking his tally of goals for the club to 59 in 92 first team outings, he was forced to retire from the game.

DONE, CYRIL

Cyril Done began his league career with Liverpool and made his first team debut on 2 September 1939, the day before war broke out and even scored in Liverpool's 1-0 victory over Chelsea at Anfield. It was to be the last league game he would play for seven years. When peacetime football resumed in 1946-47, he made 17 appearances as the Reds captured the League Championship. During the hostilities he had been a prolific scorer and though his scoring instinct seemed to have left him, he did score 37 goals in 109 games over the next six years before joining Tranmere Rovers in 1952.

Done made his debut for the Prenton Park club in a goalless home draw against Oldham Athletic on the opening day of the 1952-53 season. He ended the campaign as the club's top scorer with 26 goals including hat-tricks against Workington (Home 3-0) and Wrexham (Home 4-2). In 1953-54 he headed the club's scoring charts again, this time with 32 goals. Included in the total were hat-tricks against Wrexham (Home 6-1) and Accrington Stanley (Home 5-1). The Peel Park club suffered at the hands of Cyril Done again the following season when he netted another hat-trick against them in a 3-1 home win. Though he left Tranmere in December 1954 to join Port Vale, he was still that season's leading scorer with 17 goals. All told, big Cyril scored 75 goals in 97 games for Tranmere.

At Port Vale, he was the club's leading scorer and netted all four goals for the Valiants in a 4-3 win over Liverpool. Despite a series of injuries he was still the club's top marksman but after scoring 34 goals in 52 league games he was given a free transfer and joined Winsford United before ending his involvement with the game as player-manager of Skelmersdale United.

DRAWS

Tranmere Rovers played their greatest number of drawn league matches in a single season in 1970-71 when 22 of their matches ended all-square and their fewest in season's 1928-29 and 1984-85 when only three of their matches were drawn.

Whilst Rovers' Full Members Cup tie against Newcastle United on 1 October 1991 ended all-square at 6-6, the club's highest scoring draw in the league is 4-4, a scoreline in four matches – Southport (Away 1929-30); York City (Home 1929-30); Hull City (Home 1957-58); and York City (Home 1976-77).

DYSON, BARRY

Barry Dyson began his career with Bury but having failed to make the grade, joined Tranmere Rovers. He made his debut in a 4-2 defeat at Lincoln City on the opening day of the 1962-63 season, ending the campaign with 13 goals in 39 games. Originally a winger, he was switched to inside-forward and in 1963-64 he topped the club's scoring charts with 30 goals in 49 League and Cup games. The following season he netted his first hat-trick for the club in the opening game of the campaign as Halifax Town were beaten 5-2 in front of a Prenton Park crowd of 7,800. He ended the season with 29 goals, again heading the Rovers' scoring charts. He topped the charts for a third successive season in 1965-66 when his total of 31 goals in 42 games included another hat-trick as Tranmere beat Rochdale 5-3 at Spotland. Dyson went on the transfer list at his own request and in September 1966 after scoring 106 goals in 183 League and Cup games, he left to join Crystal Palace for a fee of £15,000. In October 1967, he moved to Watford where he scored 19 goals in 38 league games before joining Leyton Orient. He helped the Brisbane Road club win the Third Division Championship in 1969-670 but after scoring 28 goals in 160 league games, he left to end his league career with Colchester United.

E

EARLY GROUNDS

Tranmere Rovers' first ground was Steele's Field which lay between where Parkstone Road and Temple Road now run, just to the north of Prenton Park. It was owned by Tranmere Hall Estate whose agent William Steele was the licensee of the Beekeepers Arms where the players got changed. After games had finished, the players had to walk across one of Steele's other fields which members of the Tranmere Rugby Club usually used. This ground was much flatter and better drained than the sloping pitch the football club played on. In 1887, they offered the landlord £5 10 shillings (£5.50) rent, thus gazumping the rugby players who were not very pleased. Rovers were unconcerned about the controversy and erected a fence around the field of a ground they were to use for the next 25 years.

Over the years, this new ground was referred to by several names. Though it was officially called Borough Road, it was also known as Devonshire Park, South Road and Ravenshaw Field after Ann Ravenshaw who had replaced Steele. In 1895, the ground was renamed Prenton Park, even though it wasn't in Prenton!

In 1902, Rovers rented their ground to Birkenhead Warriors who brought with them a 250 seat stand which the football club kept even after the rugby club disbanded four years later. The stand was replaced in 1909 by an 800-seat stand whilst between 1907 and 1909, Rovers shared their ground yet again, this time with Cammell Laird and from 1910 with Northern Nomads.

After discovering that the ground had been sold to developers, Rovers moved across the road to the new Prenton Park, having played their last game at the ground against the Nomads in February 1912.

EASTHAM, HARRY

A member of the famous Eastham footballing family, Blackpool-born Harry Eastham began his career with his home-town club, but after failing to make the grade, left to join Liverpool. He made 63 league appearances for the Reds before joining Tranmere in the summer of 1948.

He made his Rovers' debut in a 2-1 home defeat by Hull City on the opening day of the 1948-49 season. The inside-forward's ball control and accurate passing made him a great favourite with the Prenton Park crowd. He missed very few matches in his five years with the club and in 1950-51 when the club finished fourth in the Third Division (North) he was one of three ever-presents. He went on to score 12 goals in 159 games before leaving to sign for Accrington Stanley in 1953.

After just one season with the Lancashire club, he left to play non-league football for Netherfield and Rolls Royce in the Lancashire Combination. After hanging up his boots, he became mine host at the Ainsworth Arms in Bolton, a pub occasionally frequented by the author during his youth!

EDEN, BILLY

Winger Billy Eden joined Tranmere Rovers from Darlington midway through the 1934-35 season, making his debut in a 1-0 defeat at Accrington Stanley on 16 March 1935. Over the next couple of seasons, his pin-point crosses created a number of goalscoring opportunities for Bunny Bell, Fred Urmson and Billy Woodhead. In 1937-38, when Rovers won the Third Division (North) Championship, he scored 12 goals in his 41 League and Cup appearances, including six in the last nine games of the campaign.

Eden, whose pace and trickery caused many a problem for opposing full-backs, went on to score 31 goals in 146 League and Cup games before leaving to play for New Brighton.

EGLINGTON, TOMMY

One of Everton's greatest-ever servants, Tommy Eglington missed very few games for the Blues in the 11 years after the Second World War, making 428 League and Cup appearances and scoring 82 goals. He joined Everton along with Peter Farrell from Shamrock Rovers for a joint fee of £10,000, the deal proving to be one of the best strokes of business that the Goodison club has ever pulled off.

His speed and trickery earned him 24 full caps for the Republic of Ireland and another six for Northern Ireland. He appeared alongside Peter Farrelll in the historic game at Goodison Park in 1949 when the Republic of Ireland defeated England 2-0. This was the first time England had been defeated on home soil by a non-British team. Eglington guaranteed himself a place in the pages of Everton's history when on

Tommy Eglington (centre) seen here in his Everton days.

27 September 1952 he almost single-handedly demolished Doncaster Rovers at Goodison Park by scoring five goals in a 7-1 win. A player with intricate close control and stunning shooting power, Tommy Eglington left Everton for Tranmere Rovers in 1957.

He made his debut in a 3-1 win at Chester on the opening day of the 1957-58 season and though he didn't score in that game, he ended the campaign with 14 goals in 46 appearances. In 1958-59, Eglington was ever-present though it was a campaign in which he was more of a goal maker than goalscorer. He rediscovered his shooting boots the following season and netted a hat-trick in the first game as Rovers beat Accrington Stanley 5-1. After Rovers had been relegated in 1960-61, Eglington who had scored 40 goals in 181 games returned to his native Dublin, where he now runs a butcher's shop.

EVANS, CLIVE

Clive Evans began his league career with Tranmere Rovers after joining the club as an apprentice. He made his debut in a 2-1 home win over Northampton Town in May 1977 after which he missed very few games over the next four seasons. In fact, Evans who was ever-present in season's 1977-78 and 1978-79, played in 131 consecutive league games during that period. In 1978-79 he was the club's joint-top scorer with 10 goals as they were relegated to the Fourth Division. The defensive midfield player had scored 30 goals in 200 games when he was transferred to Wigan Athletic in the summer of 1981.

After just one season at Springfield Park, he joined Crewe Alexandra but in August 1983 he was on the move again, this time to Stockport County. He spent four full seasons at Edgeley Park, playing on either side of midfield or at full-back and was outstanding during the club's relegation-haunted season of 1986-87, helping County to safety. Having scored 23 goals in 181 games, he left Stockport in September 1987 to join relegated Lincoln City where he played an important role in bringing the Imps back to Division Four. At the end of Lincoln's first season, Evans left league football having given total commitment to each of his five clubs.

EVER-PRESENTS

There have been 48 Tranmere Rovers players who have been

ever-present throughout a Football League season. The greatest number of ever-present seasons by a Rovers' player is nine by Harold Bell. Next in line is Ray Mathias who was ever-present in five seasons.

F

FA CUP

Tranmere Rovers lost their first FA Cup game in the first qualifying round on 3 October 1891 when beaten 5-1 at home by Northwich Victoria before a crowd of 2,000. Jack McKinley from the penalty-spot was the club's first cup scorer. In fact, the club didn't win an FA Cup game until 1896-97 when they won 5-1 at Warrington St Elphins. The club's biggest victory in the FA Cup is the 13-0 scoreline inflicted upon Oswestry United in October 1914.

Over the years, Rovers and Chelsea have met a number of times in cup competitions with the majority of games producing some memorable moments. In 1931-32, goals from Watts and Dixon helped Tranmere draw 2-2 at Prenton Park and though Rovers scored three goals in the replay at Stamford Bridge, Chelsea won 5-3. In 1932-33, the club reached the fourth round of the FA Cup for the first time before losing 4-0 at Leeds United in a replay. The following season, Bunny Bell scored four goals in a 7-0 win over non-league Newark Town before the club lost 3-1 to Liverpool in a fourth round tie that was switched to Anfield.

In 1951-52, Rovers needed four matches to overcome non-league Blyth Spartans before goals from Tilson and Rosenthal gave them a 2-1 victory at First Division Huddersfield Town. In the fourth round, Rovers met Chelsea at Stamford Bridge but were well beaten 4-0.

In 1952-53, Harold Atkinson netted six goals in Rovers' 8-1 win over Ashington and after Cyril Done had scored twice against Hartlepool United, the club met Tottenham Hotspur in the third round. A crowd of 21,537 saw Lloyd Iceton score for Rovers in a 1-1 draw but in the replay at White Hart Lane two days later, Spurs won 9-1 to inflict on Rovers their worst-ever FA Cup defeat. In 1956-57, Tranmere lost 2-1 to Bishop Auckland, their third FA Cup defeat at the hands of a non-league club but gained ample revenge two seasons later when Keith Williams scored four goals in an 8-1 win.

Rovers met Chelsea again in 1962-63 when a crowd of 17,162 saw the club's play out a 2-2 draw on a snow-covered Prenton Park. In the replay, Chelsea ran out winners 3-1 having been lucky to escape with a draw in the first meeting.

In 1967-68, Rovers reached the fifth round of the FA Cup for the first time in their history. George Hudson who scored a hat-trick in a 5-1 first round victory over Rochdale, scored the second goal against his former club Coventry City in a 2-0 fourth round replay success. Rovers went out in the fifth round losing 2-0 at Everton.

When Rovers drew 2-2 with Stoke City in the FA Cup fourth round of 1971-72, the tie was watched by the club's record gate of 24,424.

During the club's promotion-winning season of 1975-76, Rovers lost 2-0 at Coventry Sporting, the last time they have been beaten by a non-league club in the competition. In 1979-80 they achieved one of their best results in the FA Cup when they beat AP Leamington 9-0.

In 1997-98, the club equalled their best performance in the competition in reaching the fifth round before losing 1-0 at Newcastle United.

FARRELL, PETER

Peter Farrell's career coincided with that of Tommy Eglington. They both arrived at Everton from Shamrock Rovers in the summer of 1946 and Farrell joined Tranmere Rovers as player-manager in October 1957, four months after Eglington had joined the Prenton Park club. The Dublin-born wing-half was one of only a handful of players to appear in full internationals both for Northern Ireland and the Republic of Ireland. He represented Northern Ireland seven times when they could select players born in the Republic for the Home International Championships. He won the first two of his 28 caps for the Republic of Ireland after the war when he was still playing for Shamrock Rovers and his first with Everton against Spain in 1947. In 1949 he helped to make history when he scored one of the goals for the Republic of Ireland against England at Goodison Park. The Republic became the first non-British team to defeat England at home.

An inspiration to all around him, very popular on the field, Farrell was also something of a hero off it, mixing freely with the club's supporters in a down-to-earth manner. He captained the side for a number of years and in 11 seasons at Goodison appeared in 453 League and Cup games.

His debut for Tranmere Rovers came in a 2-1 win over Southport and his only goal for the club was the opener in a 3-2 win at Gateshead on 14 December 1957. The player-manager who appeared in 120 games in his three seasons with the club found his time at Prenton Park was not the happiest of experiences and after posts at Wrexham and Holyhead, he returned to Ireland to continue in management.

Peter Farrell, former Everton star who became Tranmere's player-manager in 1957.

FARRIMOND, SYD

Hindley-born left-back Syd Farrimond was an England Youth inter-national who, after making his debut for Bolton Wanderers in a goalless draw against Preston North End in October 1958, understud-ied Tommy Banks until winning a first team place on a regular basis in 1961-62. However, Farrimond didn't quite have the timing of the England international and his occasional vigorous tackling saw him sent-off on a number of occasions.

He was a member of the Wanderers' side for the next ten seasons, going on to appear in 404 League and Cup games for Bolton. His only goal for the club came in a 1-1 home draw against Norwich City in March 1967.

After eventually losing his place to the up and coming Don McAllister, he left Burnden Park on a free transfer following a dispute over a loyalty bonus.

He joined Tranmere Rovers and made his debut for the Prenton Park club in a goalless home draw against Torquay United in Febru-ary 1971. A firm favourite with the Rovers' supporters, he had made 153 League and Cup appearances when he left the club for coaching spells with Halifax Town, Sunderland and Leeds United.

FATHER AND SON

The only father and son to have played for Tranmere Rovers are Noel and John Kelly. Irish international Noel Kelly who joined Rovers from Nottingham Forest was the club's player-manager between 1955 and 1957. He scored seven goals in 54 first team outings before being re-placed by Peter Farrell. His son John joined the club from Cammell Laird and he scored 11 goals in 72 games before joining Preston North End. He later played for Chester, Swindon, Oldham and Walsall.

FESTIVAL OF BRITAIN

In May 1951, Tranmere Rovers played two games in the Festival of Britain, beating Dundalk 5-0 before losing 1-0 against Drumcondra.

FEWEST DEFEATS

During Tranmere's Fourth Division promotion-winning season of

1988-89, the club went through the programme of 46 matches, losing only eight games, six of them away from home. The club's first defeat was at home to Cambridge United in the sixth game of the season and then at home to York City six games later. The club's away defeats were as follows: Torquay United (2-3) Crewe Alexandra (1-2) Leyton Orient (0-2) Lincoln City (1-2) Rochdale (1-3) and Hereford United (1-2).

FINES

Tranmere Rovers cancelled their Football League match with Bolton Wanderers during the 1987-88 season in a dispute over how many police were required for the match. The League fined them £2,000 and deducted two points for failing to play the game.

FINNEY, KEN

Ken Finney played his early football with his home-town club St Helens and after a number of impressive performances, joined Stockport County in 1947. After making his Football League debut in a 3-0 defeat at Lincoln City in January 1948, he played in just nine more games in the next four seasons before winning a regular place at the start of the 1951-52 season.

Though he created a number of goalscoring chances for the likes of Jack Connor and Bill Holden, he wasn't shot-shy and in 198 League and Cup games for County, he scored 36 goals with a best of 13 in 1956-57. Also during his stay at Edgeley Park, he represented the Third Division (North) against the Southern Section on two occasions.

In March 1958, Finney left Stockport to join Tranmere Rovers and scored both the Prenton Park club's goals in a 2-0 home win over Halifax Town on his debut. He missed just one game for Rovers in 1959-60 as the club just avoided relegation to the Fourth Division. He went on to score 28 goals in 195 League and Cup games before leaving to play non-league football for Altrincham.

FIRST DIVISION

Tranmere Rovers are currently enjoying their first spell in Division One following the Football League's reorganisation in 1992-93. In that season, Rovers finished fourth but lost to Swindon Town in the divisional play-off semi-finals. Rovers qualified for the play-offs again the following season but narrowly lost to Leicester City. In 1994-95 the club reached the play-offs for the third consecutive season but went down to Reading. This was probably the club's best chance of automatic promotion but they failed to win any of their last five league games. Since then the club's best position has been 11th in 1996-97. All Rovers' fans will be hoping that 1999-2000 will be their last season in the First Division and that they win promotion to the Premier League.

FIRST LEAGUE MATCH

Tranmere Rovers played their first-ever Football League match on 27 August 1921. Their opponents at Prenton Park for this Third Division (North) match were Crewe Alexandra. A crowd of 7,011 turned out to see Rovers win 4-1 with goals from Milnes, Stuart, Groves and Ford.

FIRST MATCHES

Belmont FC played their first match against Brunswick Rovers on 15 November 1884 and won 4-0. After changing their name to Tranmere Rovers, the present club played its first-ever match against Birkenhead Argyle on 19 September 1885. The game ended all-square at 1-1 with Rovers' goal being an own goal scored five minutes from full-time by Atherton.

FISHWICK, BERT

Chorley-born Bert Fishwick was a skilful forward who played his early football with Leyland before later turning out for Hamilton Central and Chorley. He began his league career with Plymouth Argyle before later playing for Blackpool and Port Vale. Although he was a regular in the Vale side in 1927-28, he only appeared intermittently during the next three seasons and, in March 1931, he was sold to Tranmere Rovers.

He made his debut for the Prenton Park club on the final day of the 1930-31 season in a 3-0 defeat at Carlisle United. After scoring five goals in 15 games the following season, he moved to centre-half and over the next two campaigns, missed very few games. He had scored nine goals in 92 games when he left Tranmere to return to his home-town club Chorley for a second spell.

FLANAGAN, JACK

Centre-forward Jack Flanagan began his career with Manchester United but having failed to make the grade with the Old Trafford club, he joined Tranmere Rovers.

His debut for the Prenton Park club was nothing short of sensational as he netted a hat-trick in a 3-1 home win over Wigan Borough on 6 November 1926. On New Year's Day 1927, Flanagan scored five of the club's goals in a 7-2 defeat of Barrow and would have had a sixth if his shot hadn't been deflected into his own net by Barrow's Dixon. Not surprisingly, Flanagan ended the season as the club's top scorer with 26 goals in 30 games. He continued to find the net the following season, though injuries restricted his appearances to 17 in which he scored 13 goals. Included in that total was another hat-trick in a 7-3 win at Darlington.

Flanagan went on to score 43 goals in 67 first team games before leaving the club to play non-league football for Chorley.

FLOOD, EDDIE

Full-back Eddie Flood had impressed in Liverpool's Central League side for a number of seasons before joining Tranmere in 1972. He made his debut for the club in a 1-0 defeat at Watford on the opening day of the 1972-73 season and went on to score two goals in 35 games in that campaign. After missing much of the following season through a season of niggling injuries, 'Floodie' was a virtual ever-present in the Tranmere side for the next seven seasons, helping the club win promotion to the Third Division in 1975-76.

He went on to score seven goals in 350 League and Cup games for Rovers before the club gave him a free transfer at the end of the 1980-81 season.

Flood joined York City but after just 15 league appearances for the Bootham Crescent club, he was forced to retire from the game due to an arthritic knee.

FLOODLIGHTS

The Prenton Park floodlights were first switched on for the Third Division (North) match against Rochdale on 29 September 1958. For the record, a crowd of 16,878 saw Rovers win 2-1 with Keith Williams' header and an own goal by Ferguson settling the match in Tranmere's favour. These floodlights were replaced by a new set costing in the region of £70,000 and switched on in September 1988 for the match against Colchester United.

FOOTBALL LEAGUE CUP

With the exception of 1993-94 when the club reached the semi-finals, Tranmere Rovers have failed to make much impact upon the League (later Milk, Littlewoods, Rumbelows, Coca Cola and Worthington) Cup.

The club's first game in the competition was on 24 October 1960 when they won 2-0 at Port Vale with goals from Onyeali and Eglington. There followed a 2-0 home win over Crewe before Rovers were beaten 4-0 by Everton in front of a Prenton Park crowd of 14,976. In 1961-62, Alan Arnell scored the club's first hat-trick in the competition but Rovers lost 6-3 at home to Middlesborough. In 1968, Tranmere needed three matches to dispose of Chester but then again went out of the competition to Everton, losing 4-0 at Goodison Park.

There is no doubt that the highlight of the club's early League Cup history was the 1-0 defeat of high-flying Arsenal at Highbury on 2 October 1973. The all-important goal was scored by Eddie Loyden who smashed home Hugh McAuley's cross. In the next round, Rovers drew 1-1 at home to Wolves before losing 2-1 in the replay at Molineux.

After reaching the fourth round of the competition in season's 1988-89 and 1989-90 where they lost to Bristol City (Away 0-1) and Tottenham Hotspur (Away 0-4 after a 2-2 draw) respectively, the club, after beating Chelsea 4-2 on aggregate in 1991-92 almost made it to Wembley two seasons later.

They beat Oxford United 6-2 on aggregate with Pat Nevin netting a hat-trick in the 5-1 home leg win. John Aldridge who netted the other two goals in that win, scored two more in the 4-1 third round win over Grimsby Town. After beating Oldham Athletic 3-0, Rovers met

Nottingham Forest in the quarter-final. A Chris Malkin goal gave Tranmere a 1-1 draw at the City Ground before goals from Nevin and Thomas helped Rovers to a 2-0 home win in the replay. Rovers semi-final opponents were Aston Villa.

After beating Villa 3-1 at Prenton Park in the first leg, Rovers looked to have a good chance of reaching the Wembley final but after losing by the same score at Villa Park, they lost 5-4 on penalties after extra-time!

FOUNDATION

The club were formed as Belmont FC in 1884 and adopted their present title the following year. It was 1889 before Rovers joined their first league, the West Lancashire League. That year also saw the club's first success as they won the Wirral Challenge Cup. Ten years later the club nearly folded when almost all the players left to join Birkenhead FC. Thankfully they survived the crisis and in 1907-08 won the Combination title and six seasons later, the Lancashire Combination Championship. After having entered the Central League, they joined the Football League in 1921.

FOURTH DIVISION

Tranmere Rovers have had three spells in the Fourth Division. Their first match in the League's basement was at Aldershot on 23 August 1961 where despite a goal from Alan Arnell, Rovers lost 3-1. The club's first spell in the Fourth Division lasted six seasons and with the exception of that first campaign, they were always in the top eight before winning promotion in 1966-67. The club's second spell lasted just one season, for after their relegation in 1974-75, Rovers won promotion at the first attempt with Ronnie Moore's 34 league goals going a long way to helping them achieve their aim. The club's third and last spell in Division Four was also their longest. Following relegation in 1978-79, Rovers spent the next 10 seasons in the Fourth Division. They had to apply for re-election in 1980-81 but eventually won promotion in 1988-89 as runners-up to Rotherham United.

FREIGHT ROVER TROPHY

A competition designed solely and specifically for Associate Members of the Football League, the Freight Rover Trophy replaced the initial Associate Members Cup for the 1984-85 season.

Tranmere were drawn against Blackpool in the first round and though they lost the first leg at Bloomfield Road 2-1, goals from Williams, Clarke, Clayton and Palios gave them a 4-1 home win and a place in the second round against Burnley. In a hard fought game, Rovers and the Clarets drew 2-2 after extra-time before the Prenton Park club won 5-4 on penalties. In the Northern Area quarter-final, Tranmere lost 3-1 at Wigan Athletic with Colin Clarke, who had scored in every round, netting Rovers' goal.

In 1985-86, Tranmere won both of their group games, beating Preston North End 2-0 at Prenton Park and Bury 2-1 at Gigg Lane. In the Northern Area quarter-final, Rovers travelled to Burnden Park to play Bolton Wanderers but went down 2-1.

The following season Rovers lost both of their group games. Their 6-1 defeat at Wrexham was the biggest in this competition and though they gave a much better performance in the home match against Wigan Athletic, they lost 3-2 with both Tranmere goals being scored by Ian Muir.

FRITH, DAVID

David Frith made his Football League debut for Blackpool when he played in a 3-0 home win over Bolton Wanderers in August 1952. He had played in 35 games for the Seasiders when he left Bloomfield Road to join Tranmere in the summer of 1958.

He made his debut for the Prenton Park club in a 3-0 home win over Doncaster Rovers on the opening day of the 1958-59 season. Missing just one game in 1959-60, he played the majority of his matches for Rovers at left-back though he had a spell at right-back in 1960-61 and the early part of the following season.

Strong in the tackle and a good distributor of the ball, he went on to appear in 188 League and Cup games for Rovers before leaving the club at the end of the 1962-63 season to play non-league football for Fleetwood.

G

GALBRAITH, WALTER

After playing his early football with Clyde, Walter Galbraith joined New Brighton in 1948 before in August 1950, becoming player-manager. He lasted just a year with the Rakers as they finished bottom of the Third Division (North) and failed to gain re-election. He was signed as a player by Grimsby Town and in his first season helped the Mariners to runners-up spot in the Third Division (North). In June 1953 he became player-manager of Accrington Stanley, retiring from the playing side at the end of his first season. He stayed on as manager for another four seasons in which the club were twice runners-up and twice in third place. Because he had a policy of recruiting players from north of the border, he earned the tag of 'Mr McStanley'. Disappointed with the board's lack of ambition, he resigned to become manager of Bradford Park Avenue. In January 1961, he quit the Yorkshire club to take charge of Tranmere Rovers where he continued his policy of recruiting Scottish players. However, his best buy was John King, later to manage the club, from Bournemouth. Only in charge for 11 months, he could not prevent Rovers' relegation to Division Four and soon received a better offer to manage Hibernian.

In 1965 he returned to Park Avenue as general manager before joining Stockport County as chief scout, later becoming manager. His stay at Edgeley Pak was brief for after one season in which they finished bottom of the Third Division, he was sacked.

GARNETT, SHAUN

Central defender Shaun Garnett worked his way up through the club's ranks before making his debut as a substitute in a 3-0 win at Newport County in April 1988. Though he didn't play at all the following season and made only nine appearances in 1989-90, Garnett won a regular place towards the end of the 1990-91 campaign, appearing in the play-off final win over Bolton Wanderers. There followed loan spells at Chester City, Preston North End and Wigan Athletic before he joined Swansea City for £200,000 in March 1996.

Garnett, who had appeared in 146 games for Rovers struggled to find his form at the Vetch Field and in September 1996 moved to

Oldham Athletic for a fee of £150,000. Totally committed to the Boundary Park club's cause, he has at the time of writing, appeared in almost 100 games for the Latics.

Shaun Garnett shows his strength in the air.

GOALKEEPERS

Tranmere Rovers FC has usually been extremely well served by its goalkeepers and most of them have been highly popular with the supporters.

The club's first outstanding 'keeper was Arthur Briggs who joined Rovers from Hull City in 1924. He was ever-present in two seasons and appeared in 246 games before leaving to play for Swindon Town. Welsh international 'keeper Bert Gray who had played for Oldham Athletic and Manchester City before arriving at Prenton Park, won three caps whilst with Rovers and played in 213 League and Cup games. George Payne was until recently the oldest player to line-up in a Rovers' league side. One of the greatest 'keepers to play for Tranmere, he appeared in 467 games in 15 seasons with the club. Having started his league career with Blackburn Rovers, Harry Leyland joined Rovers in 1960 after appearing in the FA Cup Final for the Ewood Park club. He played in 194 games before leaving to become player-manager of Wigan Athletic. Ever-present in his first two seasons at Prenton Park, Jim Cumbes played in 156 games for Rovers before finding fame with Aston Villa. Scottish international Tommy Lawrence who moved across the water after playing in 387 games for Liverpool was the club's first choice 'keeper for two and a half seasons following his transfer in September 1971. He was replaced by Dickie Johnson who, after helping Rovers win promotion in 1975-876, went on to appear in 397 League and Cup games for the club. Eric Nixon joined Tranmere from Manchester City in 1988 for £60,000 and over the next seven years, he was a virtual ever-present. He helped the club win promotion on two occasions and beat Bristol Rovers in the Leyland DAF Cup Final. He appeared in 440 games before leaving Prenton Park to play for Stockport County.

GOALS

The most goals Tranmere Rovers have ever scored in a league game was their 13-4 victory over Oldham Athletic on Boxing Day 1935.

Bunny Bell scored nine of the goals and Billy Woodward two. The other scorers were Willie MacDonald and Fred Urmson whilst bell also missed a penalty!

GOALS – CAREER BEST

The highest goalscorer in the club's history is Ian Muir, who between season 1985-86 and the end of season 1994-95 had netted 180 goals for the club. These comprised 142 league goals, 14 FA Cup goals, six League Cup goals and 18 in other cup competitions.

GOALS – INDIVIDUAL

Bunny Bell scored nine goals in Rovers' 13-4 win over Oldham Athletic on Boxing Day 1935, whilst both Pongo Waring and Harold Atkinson have netted six goals. Waring scored six in the 11-1 defeat of Durham City in January 1928 whilst Atkinson bagged his six in the 8-1 first round FA Cup victory over Ashington in November 1952.

GOALS – SEASON

The club's highest league goalscorer in any one season remains Bunny Bell who scored 35 league goals as Tranmere finished seventh in the Third Division (North) in 1933-34. He also scored five goals in the FA Cup to take his season's tally to 40 – a total equalled by John Aldridge in 1991-92, although his number of league goals was only 22.

Bell scored four goals in the victory over Barnsley (Home 5-2) and hat-tricks against Chester (Home 6-1) Crewe Alexandra (Home 5-1) York City (Home 3-0) and Halifax Town (Home 3-2). He also scored four goals in a 7-0 FA Cup win over Newark Town.

GOALSCORING RECORDS

In 1930-31 when Rovers scored 111 goals in finishing fourth in the Third Division (North) they had for the only time in their history, three players that each scored 20 or more league goals for the club. They were Jack Kennedy (35) Ernie Dixon (31) and Farewell Watts (27).

GRAY, BERT

One of the club's greatest-ever goalkeepers, Bert Gray was already an established Welsh international when he arrived at Prenton Park in 1931. A goalkeeper whose tremendous reach, agility and courage were the principal features of his play, he began his league career with Oldham Athletic and after winning his first cap against England in 1924 went on to make 98 league appearances for the Latics before joining Manchester City. After two seasons at Maine Road he played for Manchester Central before joining Tranmere.

He made his debut in a 3-2 defeat at York City on the opening day of the 1931-32 season and went on to be a virtual ever-present in the Rovers' side for the next five seasons, making 213 League and Cup appearances.

He was captain when Rovers beat Chester 1-0 at Sealand Road in the Welsh Cup Final of 1935 – the first major trophy the club had won. After being overlooked for the manager's job after the departure of Jackie Carr, he left Prenton Park to play for Chester where he took his total of international appearances to 24.

GUBBINS, RALPH

Ellesmere Port-born forward Ralph Gubbins began his league career with Bolton Wanderers and made his debut in the final game of the 1952-53 season as Nat Lofthouse scored a hat-trick in a 3-2 win at Newcastle United. It was another three seasons before he began to play for the club on a regular basis, scoring six goals in 34 games as the Wanderers finished eighth in Division One. After losing his place to Brian Birch, Gubbins found himself understudying all of the Wanderers' forwards and in March 1958 replaced Nat Lofthouse in the FA Cup semi-final against Blackburn Rovers at Maine Road. Though he scored both Bolton's goals in a 2-1 win, there was no place for him in the Cup Final side and in October 1959 after scoring 18 goals in 101 games, he joined Hull City.

After just one and a half years at Boothferry Park in which he scored 10 goals in 45 league games he returned to the north-west to play for Tranmere Rovers. He scored twice on his debut in March 1961 as Rovers beat Colchester United 7-2 and in 1961-62, netted 21 goals in 40 games as he formed an effective striking partnership with Alan Arnell. He went on to score 37 goals in 115 games for Tranmere before leaving to play non-league football for Wigan Athletic. In his one season at Springfield Park he helped the Latics win the Cheshire League Championship, with six of his seven goals coming from the penalty-spot.

GUEST PLAYERS

The 'guest' system was used by all clubs during the war years. Although at times it was abused almost beyond belief (in that some sides that opposed Tranmere had ten or 11 'guests') it normally worked sensibly and effectively to the benefit of players, clubs and supporters alike. The most distinguished player to 'guest' for Tranmere Rovers was England centre-forward Tommy Lawton who played in a 2-2 draw at Crewe Alexandra in February 1940.

H

HAMILTON, BRYAN

A terrier-like midfield player, Bryan Hamilton began his Football League career with Ipswich Town after moving there from Linfield. He went on to score 56 goals in 199 games for the Portman Road club before signing for Everton for £40,000 in November 1975. Over the next two seasons he played in 54 games and appeared in the 1977

League Cup Final against Aston Villa. He will always be remembered for scoring the goal that never was! In the FA Cup semi-final against Liverpool, the game stood at 2-2 when with just seconds remaining, Hamilton hammered the ball past Ray Clemence's despairing dive. For no reason whatsoever, referee Clive Thomas ruled out the Irishman's effort and Liverpool went on to win the replay 3-0. Hamilton later played for Millwall and Swindon Town before joining Tranmere Rovers as player-manager.

Bryan Hamilton: Northern Ireland international who went on to become Tranmere's player-manager.

He made his debut as a substitute in a 3-0 home win over Wimbledon in October 1980 and went on to score six goals in 129 games. He made his final appearance in November 1983 but remained in charge at Prenton Park until February 1985 when he was sacked. He had steered Rovers through a number of crises before his departure. He then joined Wigan and led the Latics to Wembley success in the Freight Rover Trophy final before taking charge of Leicester City. He returned to Springfield Park in 1988 but lost his job in 1993. Capped 50 times by Northern Ireland, he became the national manager until replaced by Lawrie McMenemy in 1998.

HARVEY, JIMMY

Jimmy Harvey joined Arsenal from Glentoran in the summer of 1977 for £30,000. At that time, he was regarded as one of the best young players to have emerged from Northern Ireland for many years. In fact, he was voted the Young Player of the Year for season 1976-77. However, during his three years at Highbury, he only managed to play in three league games before being granted a free transfer to Hereford United in March 1980. He scored 39 goals in 278 league appearances for the Edgar Street club before joining Bristol City. Unable to settle at Ashton Gate, he had a loan spell with Wrexham before signing for Tranmere Rovers in October 1987. He made a goalscoring debut in a 6-1 home win over Rochdale and over the next five seasons missed very few games, being ever-present in 1989-90. He helped Rovers win promotion to the Third Division in 1988-89 and win the Leyland DAF Cup the following season. He went on to score 19 goals in 239 League and Cup games before leaving Prenton Park to join Crewe Alexandra. His stay at Gresty Road was short and he moved to Chester where he ended his league career.

HAT-TRICKS

The first players to score hat-tricks for the club were Buckley, Lee and Littler who all netted three times during a 10-0 win over Liverpool North East on 26 September 1885.

The first player to score a hat-trick for Tranmere in a Football League game was Charlie Cunningham who scored four goals in a 7-0 home win over Rochdale on 15 October 1921.

Only two players have scored hat-tricks on their debuts for Tranmere. They are Jack Flanagan in a 3-1 win over Wigan Borough on 6 November 1926 and Billy Woodward in a 5-0 home win over Southport on the opening day of the 1933-34 season.

Though Pongo Waring in an 11-1 win over Durham City in 1927-28 and Harold Atkinson in an 8-1 defeat of Ashington in 1952-53 have both scored double hat-tricks, Bunny Bell is the only player to score a triple hat-trick in English League football. He scored nine of Tranmere's goals in the 13-4 win over Oldham Athletic on Boxing Day 1935. Bell has also netted the most hat-tricks for Rovers with 12, followed by John Aldridge with nine.

HICKSON, DAVE

Dave Hickson first attracted the attention of Everton manager Cliff Britton as a free-scoring teenager with non-league Ellesmere Port but after crossing the Mersey to join the Goodison Park club in the summer of 1948, his progress was halted by National Service. Two years later, he returned to an Everton side that had been relegated to the Second Division. After making his debut at Leeds, he soon claimed a regular place in the Blues' line-up, linking effectively with John Willie Parker. Hickson earned himself a place in Everton folklore during the club's stirring run to the 1953 FA Cup semi-finals. In the fifth round tie with Manchester United he scored the winner after leaving the field to have five stitches put in a gashed eyebrow and in the quarter-final at Villa Park he scored the only goal of the game with a scorching drive from just inside the penalty area. In 1953-54, he scored 25 league goals including a hat-trick in a 4-2 win at Stoke. After one more season of top flight football he was sold to Aston Villa but after failing to settle in the Midlands, joined Huddersfield Town. He later returned to Goodison to take his tally of goals in his two spells to 111 in 243 appearances before crossing Stanley Park to join Liverpool. Twelve months later he went into non-league football with Cambridge City before after a brief spell with Bury, he joined Tranmere Rovers in the summer of 1962.

He made his debut in a 6-1 home win over Hartlepool United and though he failed to score, he ended the season as the club's top goalscorer with 23 goals in 37 games including a hat-trick in a 4-1 home win over Chesterfield. He went on to score 25 goals in 52

League and Cup appearances before returning to his first-ever club Ellesmere Port, where he ended his career.

HIGGINS, DAVE

Central defender Dave Higgins joined Tranmere Rovers on a free transfer from Eagle FC in the summer of 1983 and made his debut on 17 September 1983 in a 1-0 defeat at Mansfield Town. He spent two seasons at Prenton Park before being given a free transfer and joining South Liverpool. He later played for Caernarfon Town and it was from here that he returned to play for Tranmere again in July 1987.

In his second spell with the club, Higgins was a first team regular for 10 seasons and helped the club win promotion as runners-up to Rotherham United in 1988-89 and via the play-offs in 1990-91. He also helped the club win the Leyland DAF Cup in 1990 but he missed the final.

A great man-marker, Dave Higgins went on to appear in 434 first team games in his two spells with the club. He was also a great crowd favourite because of his committed approach to the game. Dave was granted a well-deserved testimonial game after being given a free transfer by the club.

HILL, STEVE 'MANDY'

Blackpool-born winger 'Mandy' Hill joined his home-town club with a reputation as a prolific goalscorer. He was fast and possessed a deceptive body swerve. The management at Bloomfield Road groomed him as a potential successor to Stanley Matthews and it was whilst deputising for the maestro that he made his Football League debut against Manchester City in October 1959. However, it was only in 1961-62 after Matthews had left for Stoke, that Hill won a regular place in the Blackpool side, his performances earning him four appearances in the England Under-23 side. After a series of niggling injuries and losing his place to Leslie Lea, Hill, who had made 85 appearances for the Seasiders, joined Tranmere for a then club record fee of £7,500.

He made his debut in a 4-0 home win over Chesterfield in September 1964 and, over the next four seasons, proved himself to be a valuable member of the Rovers' side. After the club had finished fifth in seasons' 1964-65 and 1965-66, Hill helped them win promotion to the Third Division in 1966-67. He went on to score 10 goals in 142 League and Cup games before leaving Prenton Park at the end of the following season.

HOME MATCHES

Tranmere's best home wins are the 13-4 defeat of Oldham Athletic in a Third Division (North) match on Boxing Day 1935 and the 11-1 victory over Durham City in a Third Division (North) match on 7 January 1928. The club's worst home defeat is 9-3, a scoreline inflicted upon them by Manchester City on Boxing Day 1938.

Tranmere have scored nine goals in a home match on three occasions: Rochdale 9-1 (Division Three (North) 1931-32) Accrington Stanley 9-0 (Division Three 1958-59) and AP Leamington 9-0 (FA Cup 1979-80).

HOME SEASONS

Though Tranmere Rovers have not gone through a complete league season with an undefeated home record, there have been three occasions when they have lost just one home match – 1927-28; 1931-32 and 1964-65.

The club's highest number of home wins in a league season is 20. This was achieved in 1964-65 from 23 matches as they finished fifth in Division Four.

HUDSON, GEORGE

After making his league debut for Blackburn Rovers, George Hudson played for Accrington Stanley and Peterborough United before Coventry City manager Jimmy Hill paid a club record fee of £21,000 to take him to Highfield Road. The Manchester-born centre-forward netted a hat-trick on his debut for the Sky Blues as Halifax Town were beaten 5-4. In 1963-64 he scored hat-tricks in three consecutive games and he ended the season with 28 goals in 36 games as Coventry won the Third Division Championship. He went on to score 75 goals in 129 games for City before being sold to Northampton Town who were then in the First Division. Within a year, Hudson had joined Tranmere Rovers for £15,000 and scored on his debut in January 1967 in a 4-1 win at Exeter City. That season he scored six goals in 18 games, helping the club win promotion to the Third Division.

In December 1967 he scored his only hat-trick for the club in a 5-1 first round FA Cup tie at home to Rochdale but at the end of the following season after scoring 22 goals in 64 games, he left the first-class game.

HUGHES, MARK

Former Welsh Youth central defender Mark Hughes began his league career with Bristol Rovers after joining them as an apprentice. He turned professional in February 1980 and Terry Cooper gave him his league debut three months later. Loaned to Torquay United, he joined Swansea City in July 1984 before being reunited with Cooper at Ashton Gate in February 1985. He featured prominently in Bristol City's promotion-challenge that season but after 22 appearances was sold to Tranmere Rovers for £3,000 in September 1985.

He made his Tranmere debut in a 3-0 home win over Aldershot and was a regular member of the Prenton Park club's side for almost nine seasons. A key figure in Rovers' rise from the Fourth Division, he also won a Leyland DAF Cup winners' medal in 1990. He featured in the club's 1993-94 Coca-Cola Cup run, scoring in the semi-final first leg as Rovers beat Aston Villa 3-1. He went on to score 12 goals in 344 League and Cup games before signing for Shrewsbury Town in the summer of 1994.

Sadly after just 27 first team appearances for the Gay Meadow club, the Port Talbot-born player had to announce his retirement from the game through injury.

HUNDRED GOALS

Tranmere Rovers have scored more than 100 goals in a season on three occasions. The highest total is 111 goals scored in 1930-31 when they finished fourth in the Third Division (North). The club first scored over 100 league goals in 1927-28 when they netted 105 goals and achieved the feat for the last time in 1931-32 when scoring 107 goals, again both campaigns were played in the Third Division (North). The club have only ever conceded 100 goals in a season on one occasion and that was in 1960-61 when they let in 115 goals to finish 21st in the Third Division and were relegated to the Fourth Division for the first time in their history.

ICETON, LLOYD

Workington-born winger Lloyd Iceton joined Preston North End in 1938 but his hopes of playing league football for the Lilywhites were thwarted by the outbreak of the Second World War. When league football resumed after the hostilities, Iceton had joined Carlisle United and in four seasons with the Brunton Park club, scored 18 goals in 77 league games.

He joined Tranmere Rovers in June 1950 and made his debut on the opening day of the 1950-51 season when his accurate crosses helped Abe Rosenthal score four goals in a 7-2 home win over York City. An ever-present in 1951-52, he played the last of his 153 games in which he scored 22 goals in October 1954, though his last two seasons with the club had seen him drift out of regular first team football.

INTERNATIONAL PLAYERS

The club's most-capped player (i.e. caps gained while players were registered with Tranmere Rovers) is the current manager John Aldridge with 30 caps for the Republic of Ireland. The following is a complete list of players who have gained full international honours whilst at Prenton Park:

Northern Ireland		Scotland	
Jack Brown	2	Pat Nevin	14
Wales		**Republic of Ireland**	
Danny Coyne	1	John Aldridge	30
Bert Gray	3	Tommy Coyne	1
Lee Jones	1	Tom Davis	2
Tony Rowley	1	Liam O'Brien	5
Stan Rowlands	1		

IRONS, KENNY

Kenny Irons graduated through Tranmere's youth ranks before making his debut as a substitute in a 4-2 home defeat by Bury in December 1989. It was midway through the following season that the attacking midfielder established himself in Rovers' league side, helping the club win promotion to the Second Division by beating Bolton Wanderers 1-0 in the play-off final. Since then he has been a virtual ever-present and at the time of writing, has scored 67 goals in over 400 first team games.

He found his best form when new player-manager John Aldridge gave him a role operating just behind the strikers. He reads the game well and knows where the goal is! In April 1993 he netted a hat-trick in a 3-1 home win over Swindon Town and repeated the feat in 1998-99, ending the campaign with 18 goals, his best return for the club.

J

JOHNSON, DICKIE

Goalkeeper Dickie Johnson made his Rovers' debut in September 1971 and kept a clean sheet in a goalless home draw against Bolton Wanderers. He played in just three matches that season, the last the return game at Burnden Park which the Wanderers won 1-0 despite an outstanding performance by Johnson. It was 1973-74 when Johnson established himself as the club's first-choice 'keeper and though the club were relegated the following season, he was ever-present in 1975-76 when Rovers won promotion from the Fourth Division. During that campaign he kept 17 clean sheets as he did when Rovers beat Arsenal 1-0 in the 1973-74 League Cup competition, probably his best game for the club.

Johnson was also ever-present in 1979-80 and 1980-81 when he appeared in 140 consecutive games for the club. After playing in the opening three games of the 1981-82 season, he lost his place to Scott Endersby, who had joined Tranmere from Ipswich Town in the close season. He played his 397th and last game for the club in a 2-2 draw at home to Mansfield Town in December 1981 before being given a free transfer at the end of the season by Bryan Hamilton.

He had one season with Altrincham before ending his playing career with South Liverpool.

JONES, GARY

Chester-born Gary Jones scored on his Tranmere debut after coming on as a substitute for Kenny Irons in a 3-1 defeat at Millwall in November 1993. Standing 6ft 3ins and weighing 14 stone, the young giant was converted from a centre-half into a centre-forward, though in 1995-96 he had a spell in the heart of the club's midfield. During that season he appeared as a substitute for the Football League XI that drew 1-1 with the Italian Serie 'B' side at Huddersfield. After spending much of the following season on the bench as cover for John Aldridge, he returned to play on a regular basis in 1997-98, scoring 11 goals. One of the club's most versatile players, he has now scored 25 goals in 140 first team games.

JONES, TOMMY

Tommy Jones joined Tranmere from mid-Rhondda in 1926 and made his debut on Boxing Day, scoring the winning goal in Rovers' 2-1 defeat of Ashington. That season, Jones scored 11 goals in 23 games including a hat-trick in a 6-0 home win over Walsall. Able to play in all the forward positions, he more than often not partnered Ellis Rimmer, the two of them creating a host of chances for Pongo Waring. During his three seasons at Prenton Park, Jones scored 28 goals in 92 games before following Rimmer to Sheffield Wednesday.

Though he spent much of his time at Hillsborough in the Reserves, he did win his two full caps for Wales, playing against Ireland in 1931-32 and France the following season. On leaving Hillsborough he spent the 1934-35 season with Manchester United before ending his playing career with Watford.

After the Second World War he returned to Prenton Park as the club's trainer before leaving in 1953 to join Birmingham City as the St Andrew's club's reserve team coach.

JUBILEE FUND

The League Benevolent Fund was launched in 1938, fifty years after the start of the Football League to help players who had fallen on hard times. It was decided that the best way to raise funds was for sides to play local derby games without taking into account league status.

On 2 August 1938, Rovers entertained New Brighton at Prenton Park and won 6-1 and on 19 August 1939, won 2-1 at Raikes Lane to complete the 'double' over their neighbours.

K

KELLY, NOEL

Noel Kelly joined Arsenal from the Irish club Glentoran in October 1947 and after impressing in the club's reserve team, made his one and only league appearance for the Gunners against Everton at Goodison Park in February 1950. He could never establish a first team place at Highbury and subsequently joined Crystal Palace in March 1950. He later played for Nottingham Forest where he won his one Irish cap against Luxembourg in 1954 before joining Tranmere as the club's first player-manager in the summer of 1955.

He made his debut in a goalless draw at Chester on the opening day of the 1955-56 season and went on to score seven goals in 54 games. He had a fairly unsuccessful two years in charge, Tranmere finishing 16th and 23rd respectively in the Northern Section, having to apply for re-election in this latter season. He left Prenton Park in October 1957, being replaced by Peter Farrell.

KENNEDY, JACK

Though he only spent two seasons at Prenton Park, the second of which was littered with a series of injuries, Jack Kennedy proved himself to be a prolific goalscorer. He joined Rovers in the 1930 close season and made his debut for the club in the opening game of the 1930-31 season, scoring in a 3-1 win at Barrow. Forming a good partnership with Ernie Dixon, he netted three hat-tricks that campaign, the first against Rochdale in a 7-3 win. That match was the start of a sequence in which Kennedy scored 12 goals in eight consecutive league games to establish a club record. He ended the season as the club's leading scorer with 35 goals in 42 games, his other hat-tricks coming in the 4-2 defeat of Rotherham United and the 8-0 win over Accrington Stanley when he actually netted four of the goals.

Despite his injuries in 1931-32, he still managed to average a goal every other game to help Rovers maintain their position of fourth in the Third Division (North).

He had scored 45 goals in 67 League and Cup games when he left Prenton Park in the summer of 1932 to join Exeter City.

KERR, JOHN

Centre-forward John Kerr made his Tranmere debut as a substitute for Steve Peplow in a 1-1 home draw against Wigan Athletic on the opening day of the 1978-79 season. After appearing as a substitute in the club's opening four games of that campaign, it was midway through the season before he won a regular place in Rovers' starting line-up. His first goal for the club was the winner against Oxford United in February 1979. He went on to score 43 goals in 178 League and Cup games with a best of 16 in 46 games in 1981682 when he topped the club's scoring charts.

After leaving Prenton Park in August 1983, he joined Bristol City. Unable to settle at Ashton Gate, he moved back to the north-west and Stockport County and in 53 games for the Edgeley Park club, scored 17 goals including his first league hat-trick in a 5-1 home win over Chester City. In March 1985 he was transferred to Bury where he ended his league career, scoring four goals in 31 appearances for the Shakers.

KIERAN, LEN

An England 'B' international, Len Kieran signed for Rovers in September 1943 but didn't play his first game for the club until March 1948, having served in the Paratroopers. The strong-tackling left-half made his debut in a 2-0 defeat at Lincoln City after which he missed very few games for the club over the next nine seasons.

His consistent displays in the club's half-back line led to him winning international recognition and in 1950 he toured Australia with the FA. When he returned to league action with Tranmere in 1950-51, Keran was ever-present as the club finished fourth in Division Three (North). Though he only scored six goals in his 359 League and Cup games, half of his total came in that campaign, including a late winner at Halifax Town.

Following a benefit match in 1956 with Harold Lloyd and Percy Steele, Keran left Prenton Park to play non-league football with Macclesfield.

KING, ALAN

Alan King was discovered by Dave Russell whilst playing for St Hughes School. Wearing the number nine shirt, he was given his debut at Hartlepool United on 18 May 1963 and scored in a 2-0 win for Rovers. Moving to play at left-half, he went on to become a loyal servant of the club, missing very few games over the next nine seasons. He was ever-present in 1965-66 when the club finished fifth in Division Four and the following season missed just one game as the Prenton Park club won promotion to the Third Division.

King scored 38 goals in 385 games for Tranmere, many of them vital strikes and perhaps none more so than the goal that gave Rovers a 1-1 draw at Coventry City in the fourth round of the FA Cup in 1967-68.

Following a number of rows with manager Ron Yeats, he was given a free transfer and went to play non-league football for Ellesmere Port Town, Bangor and Marine.

KING, JOHN

John King first joined Everton as a 15-year-old schoolboy and made his league debut for them in a 3-1 defeat at Preston North End in October 1957. He went on to make 49 first team appearances before being transferred to Bournemouth in the summer of 1960. Seven months later he joined Tranmere Rovers for the first time and made his debut in a 2-1 win at Shrewsbury Town. Soon appointed captain, he made 264 League and Cup appearances and helped the club win promotion in 1966-67. In July 1968 he was given a free transfer and moved to Port Vale, also helping them to promotion. After drifting into non-league football with Wigan Athletic, he returned to Prenton Park in 1973 as coach.

With the departure of manager Ron Yeats in the summer of 1975, King was appointed his successor and at the end of his first season in charge, Rovers won promotion to the Third Division. But two seasons alter they were relegated and at the end of the 1979-80 season when Rovers finished 15th in the Fourth Division, King was sacked.

He joined Rochdale as coach and also managed Northwich Victoria, twice taking them to Wembley in the FA Trophy, winning once, and Caernarfon before returning to Tranmere in April 1987. The Prenton Park club finished runners-up in Division Four in 1988-89 and the following season won the Leyland DAF Cup beating Bristol Rovers in the final at Wembley. A week later they returned to Wembley but lost to Notts County in the Third Division play-off final. However, the following season they were promoted to the Second Division after beating Bolton Wanderers in the final of the play-offs at Wembley. Rovers reached the new First Division play-offs for three consecutive seasons but failed to win a place in the Premier League. In April 1996, John King, who has been a terrific servant of the club, was relieved of his duties and moved upstairs to become 'Director of Football'.

KNOWLES, JIM

Jim Knowles, who had worked as a film extra at Elstree Studios was appointed as assistant-secretary to Bert Cooke at Prenton Park in 1931. When Cooke was sacked in 1935, Knowles was promoted to secretary and held that position throughout Jack Carr's reign as manager. When Carr left the club, Knowles took over the dual role of secretary and manager, despite having had no experience as either a player or a manager.

He steered Rovers to the Third Division (North) title in 1937-38 – the only divisional championship success in the club's history. They struggled in the Second Division the following season and in January 1939, Knowles left the club.

L

LARGEST CROWD

It was on 5 February 1972 that Prenton Park housed its largest crowd. The occasion was the FA Cup fourth round match against Stoke City.

A crowd of 24,424 saw the Rovers draw 2-2 with goals from Ron Yeats and Ken Beamish.

LATE FINISHES

Tranmere Rovers' final match of the season against Wrexham at the Racecourse Ground on 14 June 1947 is the latest date for the finish of any of the Prenton Park club's seasons. A crowd of 2,974 saw the teams play out a goalless draw.

LAWRENCE, TOMMY

When Bill Shankly arrived at Anfield in 1959, Tommy Lawrence was lingering in the reserves. He soon promoted him and the Scotsman went on to make 387 appearances for the club. Affectionately known by the Kopites as the 'Flying Pig', Lawrence was never a spectacular goalkeeper but was always dependable. The underrated 'keeper won international recognition for Scotland in June 1963 when he played against the Republic of Ireland. The following season brought a League Championship medal but the arrival of Ray Clemence spelled the end to Lawrence's Anfield career and in September 1971 he joined Tranmere Rovers.

He made his debut in a 3-2 defeat at Halifax Town but kept his place for the rest of the season, missing just two of the club's last 44 games. He was the club's first-choice 'keeper for the next two-and-a-half seasons when he turned in a number of memorable performances. He had appeared in 94 League and Cup games for Rovers when he left Prenton Park to play non-league football for Chorley.

LEADING GOALSCORERS

Tranmere Rovers have provided the Football League's divisional leading goalscorer on five occasions. They are:

1935-36	Bunny Bell	Third Division (North)	33 goals
1975-76	Ronnie Moore	Fourth Division	34 goals
1984-85	John Clayton	Fourth Division	31 goals
1994-95	John Aldridge	First Division	24 goals
1995-96	John Aldridge	First Division	27 goals

LEAGUE GOALS – CAREER HIGHEST

Ian Muir holds the Prenton Park record for the most league goals with a career total of 142 between 1985 and 1995.

LEAGUE GOALS – LEAST CONCEDED

During the 1937-38 season, Tranmere conceded just 41 goals in 42 games when winning the Third Division (North) Championship.

LEAGUE GOALS – MOST INDIVIDUAL

Jack Kennedy holds the Tranmere Rovers record for the most league goals scored in a season with 35 scored in 1930-31 when the Prenton Park club finished fourth in the Third Division (North).

LEAGUE GOALS – MOST SCORED

Tranmere's highest goals tally in the Football League was during the Third Division (North) campaign of 1930-31 when they scored 111 goals.

LEAGUE VICTORY – HIGHEST

Tranmere Rover's best league victory was the 13-4 win over Oldham Athletic at Prenton Park on Boxing Day 1935. Bunny Bell scored nine of the goals and Billy Woodward two whilst the club's other scorers were Willie MacDonald and Fred Urmson.

On 7 January 1928, Tranmere beat Durham City 11-1 with Pongo Waring scoring six of the goals and Harry Littlehales two. Rovers other scorers were Bert Cartman and Tommy Jones and an own goal by a Durham defender.

LEWIS, JACK

Welsh international wing-half Jack 'Ginger' Lewis began his career with his home-town club Newport County. After two seasons with the Somerton Park club, he moved to Cardiff City and though he failed to establish himself in the Bluebirds' side, he did win a Welsh cap against Scotland in October 1925. Lewis was in the Cardiff party going to play a league fixture at Aston Villa when he was told to change trains at Newport and report to Ninian Park where Wales had a selection problem, and he was required to play.

Nicknamed 'Ginger' for obvious reasons, he joined Tranmere Rovers in March 1926 and made his debut in a 2-0 home win over Crewe Alexandra. He was ever-present the following season as Rovers finished the campaign ninth in the Third Division (north). Over the next seven seasons, Lewis missed very few games, making 288 first team outings before hanging up his boots at the end of the 1933-34 season.

LEYLAND, HARRY

Goalkeeper Harry Leyland began his Football League career with Everton but in five seasons at Goodison Park he had made only 36 appearances when he was released in the summer of 1956. Unable to find a new league club, he was on his way to join non-league Tonbridge with team-mate Ron Saunders when Blackburn manager Johnny Carey swooped to sign Leyland as a replacement for Reg Elvy.

An agile and brave 'keeper, he was ever-present when the Ewood Park club won promotion to the First Division in 1957-58 and won an FA Cup runners-up medal in 1960. It was during that 1959-60 campaign that he began to show his vulnerability to injury and early the following season after appearing in 188 games, he joined Tranmere Rovers.

He made his debut on 18 March 1961 as Rovers were beaten 4-1 at Grimsby Town and over the next five seasons missed very few games being ever-present in seasons 1964-65 and 1965-66 when he appeared in 98 consecutive games. The club finished fifth in Division Four in each of these seasons, just missing out on a promotion place.

He went on to play in 194 League and Cup games before bowing out of league football to join Wigan Athletic where he became player-manager.

LEYLAND DAF CUP

The Leyland DAF Cup replaced the Sherpa Van Trophy for the 1989-90 season. Tranmere won both group matches, beating Chester 1-0 at Prenton Park and Rochdale 1-0 at Spotland with Ian Muir scoring the winner on each occasion. After beating Scunthorpe United

2-1 in the first round, goals from McNab, Morrissey and Muir helped them beat Chester 3-0 and take Rovers through to the Northern Area semi-final where they met Bolton Wanderers. Though the Trotters had beaten Rovers 3-1 at Prenton Park in the league the previous month, goals from Steele and Muir gave Tranmere victory and a place in the two-legged Northern Area final against Doncaster Rovers. In the first leg at Prenton Park, Malkin and Muir scored for Tranmere in a 2-0 win, whilst Muir netted for Rovers at Belle Vue in a 1-1 draw. In the final at Wembley in front of a crowd of 48,402, Tranmere played the Third Division Champions Bristol Rovers. Ian Muir opened the scoring and though Devon White equalised for the Pirates, Jim Steel netted a late winner to give Rovers the trophy.

Tranmere's first game in defence of the trophy in 1990-91 saw them lose 1-0 at Bolton Wanderers but then a 4-0 win at home to Blackpool where Ian Muir (2) Johnny Morrissey and Jim Steel were the scorers, saw the club enter the knockout stages were they were drawn at home to Rotherham United in the first round. A comfortable 3-0 win over the Millmoor club took Rovers through to the Northern Area quarter-final where goals from Muir and Thomas gave them a 2-0 win. In the semi-final, two goals from Muir and another from Jim Steel gave Tranmere a 3-0 win at Springfield Park against a disappointing Wigan Athletic side. Ian Muir was in devastating form in the first leg of the Northern Area final against Preston North End at Prenton Park, netting a hat-trick in a 4-0 win. Despite losing the second leg at Deepdale 1-0, Rovers went through to Wembley for the second year in succession where they played Birmingham City. A crowd of 58,756 saw the Midlands side take a 2-0 lead but goals from Steve Cooper and Jim Steel levelled the scores before a late goal from John Gayle took the trophy to St Andrew's.

LITTLEHALES, HARRY

Inside-forward Harry Littlehales joined Tranmere Rovers from Reading in the summer of 1923 and made his league debut for the club in a 3-0 home win over Barrow in the seventh match of the 1923-24 season. His first four seasons at Prenton Park saw him in and out of the Rovers' side and it was only in 1927-28 that he established himself as a first team regular. That campaign saw him have his best season for there club in terms of goals scored, as he netted 15 goals in 38 games.

He continued to find the net the following season when his total of 13 goals in 41 first team outings included four in the 6-1 demolition of Nelson in November 1928.

In 1929-30, Littlehales moved to wing-half to accommodate Reg Cropper who had joined the club from Guildford City but after taking his tally of goals to 52 in 173 League and Cup games, he left to join Wrexham. But after just two league appearances for the Robins, the Burslem-born player left the game.

LIVERPOOL SENIOR CUP

Tranmere Rovers have won the Liverpool Senior Cup on seven occasions, the first being in 1933-34 when they won 4-1 at New Brighton. The Rakers were Tranmere's opponents when they won the trophy for a second time in 1948-49, Rovers winning 3-1. Rovers' third success in the Liverpool Senior Cup the following season was also against New Brighton but this time the tie was played over two legs with Rovers winning 5-0 on aggregate. The club's fourth success came in 1954-55 when Southport were beaten 2-0. In 1969-70, Rovers should have met Liverpool in the final but the Reds conceded a walkover! They did beat Liverpool 2-1 in the 1972-73 competition to win the trophy for a fifth time and then defeated Everton 3-1 the following year to retain the trophy. The club last won the trophy in 1994-95 when they beat Marine 2-0.

One of the most exciting finals Rovers were ever involved in was the 1958-59 encounter with Everton. Keith Williams scored a hat-trick for Tranmere but the Blues ran out winners 8-5.

LLOYD, HAROLD

Goalkeeper Harold Lloyd joined Tranmere Rovers from his home-town club Flint Town in 1945 and made his league debut in the opening game of the 1946-47 season when Rovers lost 4-1 at home to Rotherham United. He went on to appear in 39 games that season but over the next ten seasons, shared the goalkeeping duties with George Payne. In 1951-52, Lloyd missed just one of the club's league matches, his performances almost earning him selection for Wales at full international level.

Lloyd stayed at Prenton Park until 1957 when, after appearing in 202 first team games, he left to play non-league football for Runcorn.

LOWEST

The lowest number of goals scored by Tranmere Rovers in a single league season is 39 in 1938-39 when the club finished bottom of the Second Division and were relegated. The club's lowest points record in the League also occurred in that 1938-39 season when Rovers gained just 17 points!

LOYDEN, EDDIE

Liverpool-born centre-forward Eddie Loyden began his league career with Blackpool but after just two appearances he was allowed to join Carlisle United. He found it difficult to break into the first team at Brunton Park and moved on to Chester without making a single league appearance for the Cumbrian side.

His one season at Sealand Road saw him score 22 goals in 37 league games but the club finished third from bottom of the Fourth Division and had to apply for re-election. Loyden moved on to Shrewsbury Town and later Barnsley before returning to Chester for a second spell in November 1970. He took his tally of league goals to 48 in 99 games before signing for Tranmere Rovers in the summer of 1972.

Though he failed to score on his debut on the opening day of the 1972-73 season as Rovers lost 1-0 at Watford, he ended the campaign as the club's top scorer with 19 goals including a hat-trick in a 4-0 home win over Charlton Athletic.

He went on to score 25 goals in 69 games for Rovers before leaving to play non-league football with Highlands Park.

LUMBY, JIM

Grimsby-born inside-forward Jim Lumby began his league career with his home-town club but after scoring 12 goals in 31 league games, left to play non-league football for Brigg Town. Scunthorpe United gave him the chance to resurrect his league career and he re-paid them by netting 28 goals in 55 outings before joining Carlisle United. After just one season with the Cumbrian club, Rovers' manager John King brought him to Prenton Park and he made his debut on the opening day of the 1979-80 season, scoring the winner in a 2-1 victory at Port Vale. Though he netted a hat-trick in the 9-0 FA Cup win over AP Leamington, generally he struggled in front of goal.

He made amends in 1980-81, topping the club's scoring charts with 18 goals in 31 games including a hat-trick in a 5-0 home win over York City, even though he left Prenton Park in January 1981 to join Mansfield Town. Lumby, who had scored 25 goals in 60 games for Rovers continued to find the net for the Stags and in a nine year career, scored 86 goals in 210 league games for his five clubs.

McDEVITT, KENNY

Liverpool-born right-winger Kenny McDevitt had been spotted playing for Unity Boys Club when Tranmere Rovers signed him in January 1950. He made his debut for the Prenton Park club in a Third Division (North) game at Barrow on Boxing Day 1951, a match which Rovers lost 2-0.

Though McDevitt created many goals for his team-mates with his pin-point crosses, he scored his fair share of goals as well. In each of three seasons from 1954-55, he scored seven league goals and in the last of these, he netted his only hat-trick for the club in a 4-2 home win over Scunthorpe United.

He went on to score 40 goals in 249 League and Cup games for Tranmere before hanging up his boots at the end of the 1958-59 season.

McDONNELL, CHARLIE

Charlie McDonnell was a scheming inside-forward who also had an eye for goal. He made his debut in a 1-1 draw at Hartlepool United in September 1957 before establishing himself in the Rovers' side the following season. It was during this campaign that he scored five goals in four consecutive games, only one of which was won. He stayed at Prenton Park until the end of the 1960-61 season when he left to join Stockport County.

He continued to find the net for the Edgeley Park club, scoring 32 goals in 85 games before returning to Tranmere for a second spell in

October 1963. Injuries and a loss of form kept him out of the side for much of that season but in 1964-65 he formed a prolific partnership up front with Barry Dyson and John Manning, ending the campaign as the second-top scorer with 24 goals in 43 games. He had scored 52 goals in 118 games in his two spells with the club before leaving to end his league career with Southport.

McGREAL, JOHN

Cultured central defender John McGreal made his Tranmere debut in a 1-1 draw at Southend United in April 1992, though it was towards the end of the 1993-94 season before he established himself as a first team regular. He made 19 appearances for the club in those last few weeks of the season and scored his only goal to date for the club in a 1-1 draw at Leicester City.

Strong in the tackle, he revels in bringing the ball out of defence and has often been compared to the Liverpool and Scotland international Alan Hansen. He was appointed club captain for the 1996-97 season and though there were rumours that he was going to pursue a move to France, he stayed at Prenton Park, appearing in over 200 games for the club until joining Ipswich Town in the summer of 1999.

McNAB, NEIL

Neil McNab was only 15 years old when he played for Morton in the Scottish First Division, signing for Spurs for £40,000 in February 1974. A hard-working, gritty midfield player, it took him until 1977-78 to establish a place in the White Hart Lane club's first team. He was ever-present in the club's Second Division promotion campaign and won Scottish Under-21 honours to add to his schoolboy and youth honours. After losing his place in a Spurs midfield of Ardilles, Hoddle and Villa, he joined Bolton Wanderers for £250,000.

He then moved around, playing for Brighton, Leeds United on loan and Portsmouth on loan before a permanent move to Manchester City. He proved invaluable in helping City win promotion to the First Division in 1989.

He was sold to Tranmere Rovers in December 1989 and made his debut in a 3-1 home defeat against one of his former clubs, Bolton Wanderers. At the end of his first season, he had helped Rovers win the Leyland DAF Cup and reach the play-offs where they lost in the final to Notts County. In 1991 the club won promotion to the Second Division, though McNab missed the play-off final win over Bolton Wanderers. He went on to score eight goals in 139 games before leaving to join Ayr United.

Neil McNab, much-travelled midfielder.

MALKIN, CHRIS

Chris Malkin joined Tranmere Rovers from Stork FC in the summer of 1987 and made his debut as a substitute in a 2-1 home win over Exeter City in the fourth league match of the 1987-88 season. After helping the club win promotion the following season, he was in splendid form in 1989-90 when Rovers won the Leyland DAF Cup, scoring 24 goals in 57 games.

When Rovers won promotion via the play-offs in 1990-91, Malkin scored the only goal of the final against Bolton Wanderers at Wembley in extra-time. Malkin was a virtual ever-present for seven seasons at Prenton Park but in July 1995 after scoring 75 goals in 304 games, he joined Millwall for a fee of £400,000.

Pacy and tireless in his role up front, he scored 15 goals in 59 games for the Lions before being allowed to return to the north-west and join Blackpool in October 1996 for £275,000. His first goal for the Seasiders was against his former club but his appearances have since been restricted by injury problems and the club's record signing after just three seasons at Bloomfield Road was released at the end of the 1998-99 campaign.

Chris Malkin, scorer of the goal that helped Rovers win the play-off final in 1991.

MANAGERS

This is the complete list of Tranmere Rover's full-time managers with the inclusive dates in which they held office. Biographies of all the managers can be found in this A-Z.

Bert Cooke	1912-1935	Jackie Wright	1969-1972
Jack Carr	1935-1936	Ron Yeats	1972-1975
Jim Knowles	1936-1939	John King	1975-1980
Bill Ridding	1939-1945	Bryan Hamilton*	1980-1985
Ernie Blackburn	1946-1957	Frank Worthington*	1985-1987
Noel Kelly*	1955-1957	Ronnie Moore*	1987
Peter Farrell*	1957-1960	John King	1987-1996
Walter Galbraith	1961	John Aldridge*	1996-
Dave Russell	1961-1969		

* Appointed as player-manager

MANNING, JOHN

John Manning was playing centre-half for Liverpool Reserves when Tranmere manager Dave Russell signed him in May 1962. That was the position he played on his debut as Rovers lost 1-0 at Workington on 20 August 1962 but after just 11 appearances at centre-half, he was switched to centre-forward with devastating results. Forming a deadly goalscoring partnership with Barry Dyson, he netted 20 goals in 31 games in 1963-64 and 22 goals in 36 games in 1964-65. During this latter season, he scored his only hat-trick for the club in a 5-1 home win over Bradford City. In October 1966, he left Prenton Park at his own request, joining Shrewsbury Town for a fee of £12,000.

He scored 18 goals in 39 games for the Gay Meadow club before spells with Norwich City, Bolton Wanderers and Walsall. In March 1972 he returned to Prenton Park and took his tally of goals to 77 in 147 League and Cup games before leaving to play for Crewe Alexandra and later Barnsley. The much-travelled centre-forward scored 141 goals in 367 league games for his seven clubs.

MARATHON MATCHES

The FA Cup second round draw of 1971-72 paired Tranmere Rovers with non-league Blyth Spartans. The two sides met at Prenton Park where Rovers were grateful for an own goal by Blyth defender Sowden to give them a 1-1 draw. In the replay in the north-east four days later, the game was abandoned 13 minutes from the end of extra-time because of bad light with the score again 1-1. The next meeting was held at Brunton Park, the home of Carlisle United where two goals from Abe Rosenthal again gave Rovers a share of the spoils in a 2-2 draw. The fourth and final meeting between the two clubs took place at Goodison Park 23 days after their first game. This time Tranmere ran out winners 5-1 with their goals being scored by Tilston (2) Ray Williams, Bainbridge and Rosenthal.

When Rovers played Chester in the 1968-69 League Cup, they became the only league club to figure in ties that needed four meetings in both the FA Cup and League Cup.

MARKSMEN – LEAGUE

Tranmere Rover's top league goalscorer is Ian Muir who struck 142 league goals during his ten years at Prenton Park. Only four players have hit more than 100 league goals for the club:

1.	Ian Muir	142
2.	John Aldridge	138
3.	Bunny Bell	102
4.	Barry Dyson	100
5.	Fred Urmson	94
6.	Harold Atkinson	91
7.	Keith Williams	88
8.	Ronnie Moore	72
9.	John Manning	70
10.	George Yardley	68

MARKSMEN – OVERALL

Six players have hit a century of goals for Tranmere Rovers in all matches. The club's top marksman is Ian Muir. The Century Club consists of:

1.	Ian Muir	180
2.	John Aldridge	174
3.	Bunny Bell	113
4.	Fred Urmson	107
5.	Barry Dyson	106
6.	Harold Atkinson	104

MARTINDALE, DAVE

Liverpool-born midfield player Dave Martindale began his career with Caernarfon Town before signing for Tranmere Rovers in the summer of 1987. A wholehearted player, he made his debut for the Prenton Park club in a 3-0 defeat at Scunthorpe United on the opening day of the 1987-88 season, a campaign in which he scored five goals in 38 games. The following season he helped the club win promotion to the Third Division as they finished runners-up to Rotherham United, against whom both games were goalless draws. In 1989-90, Martindale helped the club reach Wembley in both the Leyland DAF Cup and the play-offs but didn't appear in either match! The club were back at Wembley on two occasions in 1990-91 and after coming on as a substitute in the Leyland DAF Cup Final against Birmingham City he was in the starting line-up for the play-off final against Bolton Wanderers which Rovers won 1-0.

He went on to score 12 goals in 212 games for Tranmere before leaving the club to join Doncaster Rovers, where injuries forced his retirement without him playing in a first team game.

MATCH OF THE DAY

Tranmere Rover's first appearance on BBC's 'Match of the Day' was on 9 January 1965 when they lost 1-0 at Oxford United in a Fourth Division match. The only goal of the game was scored by Cyril Beavon, from the penalty-spot.

MATHIAS, RAY

Ray Mathias holds the club record for the most League and Cup appearances, having played in 637 games over 18 seasons in the Rovers' side. He was spotted whilst playing for Ellesmere Port Town as a 15-year-old and though he joined Tranmere in December 1964 he had to wait almost four years before making his league debut in a 1-1 draw at Scunthorpe United in March 1968. Though he started his career in midfield, he was converted to full-back and over the years, missed very few games, being ever-present in five seasons. One of those seasons was 1975-76 when the club won promotion from the Fourth Division. After playing his last match for the club in a 2-0 defeat at home to Swindon Town in September 1984 he turned his hand to coaching

Ray Mathias

before being appointed assistant-manager to Bryan Hamilton at Prenton Park, following the death of Eddie Robertson. When Hamilton was dismissed in February 1985, Mathias took over as caretaker-manager but was not given the chance to do the job on a permanent basis with Bruce Osterman appointing Frank Worthington.

Mathias followed Hamilton to Springfield Park, taking over as Latics manager in June 1986. He led the club to their most successful season to date with an FA Cup run to the sixth round and to fourth place in the League and a play-off place. After a poor season with the Latics in 1988-89 he returned to Tranmere as the Training Centre Manager. He returned to Wigan where, in 1998-99, he led the club to success in the Autowindscreen Shield Final at Wembley and to the Second Division play-offs.

MERCANTILE CREDIT FESTIVAL

The Mercantile Centenary Festival took place at Wembley over the weekend of 16-17 April 1988. Qualification for the tournament was based on the number of league points won in the first 15 league games after 1 November 1987. Eight clubs came from Division One, four from Division Two and two each from the Third and Fourth Divisions. Rovers' 15 games after 1 November brought seven wins, three draws and five defeats.

A Dave Martindale goal was enough to defeat Wimbledon in the first round before goals from Morrissey and Muir helped Rovers beat Newcastle United in the quarter-final. Muir netted both goals in the semi-final against Nottingham Forest as Rovers drew 2-2 but then went out of the competition 1-0 on penalties.

MESTON, SAMMY

The son of the famous Southampton half-back, he was an immensely promising player who looked to have a fine career in front of him until he was cruelly struck by two serious injuries. Having recovered from a broken leg he appeared in 10 games for the Saints before breaking the same leg again. After this he struggled to regain fitness and joined Gillingham. He moved to Everton in 1927 but played only one league game for them before joining Tranmere.

He scored one of Rovers' goals on his debut in a 5-4 home win over Rotherham United on the opening day of the 1929-30 season. He missed very few games in three seasons at Prenton Park and was ever-present in 1930-31. He had scored 31 goals in 115 games before returning south to play for Newport on the Isle of Wight.

MILLINGTON, RALPH

After impressing Rovers' scout Tommy Jones whilst playing for Neston Nomads in a local Cup Final at Prenton Park, Ralph Millington joined Tranmere as an amateur in 1948, turning professional two years later. He made his debut on 23 August 1950 in a 2-2 draw at Bradford City and though he started as a right-half, he soon moved to centre-half where he went on to give the club 11 seasons service.

In 1951, National Service threatened to disrupt Millington's league career but he continued to keep his place in the side by travelling each week from Lichfield where he was stationed. He missed very few games and was ever-present in 1956-57 when the club finished 23rd in the Third Division (North) and had to apply for re-election.

Captain of the Rovers' side for much of his time at Prenton Park, he appeared in 381 League and Cup games before Tranmere manager Walter Galbraith gave him a free transfer at the end of the 1960-61 season. He then joined Noel Kelly at Ellesmere Port Town where he played for a further five seasons.

MOORE, RONNIE

Ronnie Moore joined Tranmere Rovers as an amateur in 1971 and made his debut in a 3-1 defeat at Oldham Athletic in November of that year. In his early days at Prenton Park, Moore was played at both

centre-half and cen-
tre-forward until he eventually settled in an attacking role
to become one of the lower divisions' leading scorers.

In the club's promo-
tion-winning season of
1975-76, Moore scored 37
goals in 50 games including
three matches (two in succession) when he scored four
goals – Brentford (Home 5-1)
Stockport County (Home 5-0)
and Newport County (Away
5-1). He also netted all three
goals in a 3-0 defeat of
Huddersfield Town. He
topped the club's scoring
charts again in 1977-78 with
17 goals and in 1978-79 was
joint-top scorer, netting another hat-trick in a 6-2 win
over Chester.

Ronnie Moore, prolific goalscorer who had two spells with the club.

It took £100,000 to prise him from Prenton Park but the goals dried up for him once he joined Cardiff City. Popular with the fans for his honest endeavours, he seemed fated never to get the goals his work-rate deserved.

He was sold to Rotherham in 1980 and he scored profusely as the Millers won promotion from the Third Division in 1980-81. After scoring 51 goals in 125 appearances he moved to Charlton Athletic but when the Londoners hit their cash crisis in 1984 he moved to Rochdale before turning his career full circle and going back to Tranmere Rovers in the Fourth Division in 1986.

He took his tally of goals to 86 in 372 games but following a three-month spell as caretaker-boss following Frank Worthington's dismissal, he resigned after a dispute over terms. He later became the club's coach.

MORETON, JIMMY

The son of Jack Moreton who played for Rovers in 1891, Jimmy Moreton gave the club 32 years service as a player and trainer after joining Rovers in 1910 from Cammel Laird. After playing in the club's reserve side for a few years his career was interrupted by the First World War but when Rovers played their first league game at home to Crewe Alexandra in August 1921, Moreton lined-up at outside-right after having joined the club as a right-half.

He was a first team regular in the club's league side for six seasons and in 1924-25 provided many of the crosses from which Dixie Dean scored his 27 goals.

Moreton went on to score 12 goals in 159 League and Cup games before following his decision to finish playing, he became the trainer alongside Bert Cooke the club's secretary-manager.

MORRISSEY, JOHNNY

Tranmere's longest-serving player, he began his league career with Everton but after just one appearance in the Blues' first team in a 2-0 defeat at Luton on the final day of the 1984-85 season, he left to join Wolves on a free transfer. He had appeared in 11 games for the Molineux club when Frank Worthington paid £8,000 to bring him to Prenton Park.

The son of the Liverpool and Everton star by the same name, he made his Rovers debut at Southend United in October 1985 where he scored one of the club's goals in a 2-2 draw. Since then he has been a virtual ever-present in the Tranmere side, helping them win the Leyland DAF Cup in 1989-90 after promotion to the Third Division the previous season. The brilliant jinking runs of the right-winger were instrumental in the club reaching the divisional play-offs on four occasions, reaching the Second Division in 1990-91 after beating Bolton Wanderers in the final. Never a prolific goalscorer, that was his best seasons in terms of goals scored as he netted 12 in 55 games. Now in his 14th season at Prenton Park, the mesmerising winger has continued to supply threatening crosses into the box and has taken his tally of goals to 63 in 558 League and Cup games.

MOST MATCHES

Tranmere Rovers played their most number of matches, 65, in season 1989-90. This comprised 46 league games, one FA Cup game, seven League Cup games, eight Leyland DAF Cup games and three play-off games.

MOTTO

The club's motto "Ubi fides ibi lux et robur" means 'Where there is faith, there is light and strength" – very appropriate when one considers that the club came close to extinction in 1982.

MUIR, IAN

With England Schoolboy honours behind him, Ian Muir joined Queen's Park Rangers but despite scoring twice on his league debut in April 1981, he played in just one more game before a brief loan spell at Burnley in October 1982. Short spells at Birmingham and Brighton followed, together with a loan spell at Swindon Town before Muir moved to Prenton Park in the summer of 1985.

After coming on as a substitute for Doug Anderson in a 3-1 defeat at Orient on the opening day of the 1985-86 season, he ended the campaign with 15 goals in 38 games including four in the 7-0 defeat of Peterborough United. For the next five seasons, Muir was the club's top scorer with a best of 35 in 65 games during 1989-90.

Muir made major contributions to two promotions from Division Four to Division Two. In 1990 he helped Tranmere to Leyland DAF Cup success, scoring freely along the way including a goal in the final against Bristol Rovers. During the 1990-91 season, Muir broke the Tranmere Rovers all-time goalscoring record held by Bunny Bell since 1936. In the summer of 1991, he was joined at Prenton Park by John Aldridge, the two of them forming a formidable pairing.

Muir went on to score 180 goals in 393 games, including five hat-tricks before in June 1995 joining Birmingham City for £125,000. Surprisingly after just one league appearance he joined Darlington on loan before returning to St Andrew's and subsequently fading from the scene completely!

MUNGALL, STEVE

A great servant to Tranmere Rovers, Steve Mungall played his early football for Chapelhall in his native Scotland before joining Motherwell in 1976. He made 48 first team appearances for the Fir Park club before moving to Prenton Park on a free transfer in the summer of 1979.

He made his Rovers' debut as a substitute for Steve Peplow in a 1-1 draw at Huddersfield Town in November 1979, going on to miss very few games over the next 16 seasons. Playing mainly at full-back, he was ever-present in 1985-86 and 1986-87 during which time he played in 135 consecutive matches. He helped the club win promotion in 1988-89 and 1990-91 and won a Leyland DAF Cup winners' medal when Bristol Rovers were beaten 2-1 in 1990.

He appeared in 624 first team games, just 13 short of Ray Mathias' club appearance record.

Mungall, who was always willing and able whenever called upon, is now the club's first team kit man.

Steve Mungall, one of the club's most popular players.

N

NEUTRAL GROUNDS

Tranmere Rovers have had to replay on a neutral ground in the FA Cup on the following occasions:

Date	Opponents	Venue	FA Cup	Score
03.01.1952	Blyth Spartans	Brunton Park	Round 2 (1R)	2-2
07.01.1952	Blyth Spartans	Goodison Park	Round 2 (2R)	5-1
30.11.1970	Scunthorpe Utd	Goodison Park	Round 1 (1R)	0-1

The club's appearances in the Leyland DAF Cup Final and Play-Off Finals at Wembley also qualify for inclusion.

NEVIN, PAT

Glasgow-born Pat Nevin began his career with Clyde before coming south of the border to join Chelsea for a fee of £95,000 in the summer of 1983. At Stamford Bridge he won the first of 28 full international caps for Scotland and scored 42 goals in 227 League and Cup games but after five distinguished years, he left the London club to sign for Everton. The two clubs were unable to agree on the size of the transfer fee and so the matter was placed before an independent tribunal which fixed the fee at £925,000. Nevin's early days at Goodison were testing, for in only his third game he damaged his knee ligaments and was sidelined for three months. Frustrated at being out of the team, he tried to come back too early but by the end of the season he had returned and scored vital goals in two Cup semi-finals. He went on to play in 138 League and Cup games for the Blues before moving across the Mersey to play for Tranmere Rovers.

He made his debut in a 2-1 home win over Port Vale in March 1992 whilst on loan before joining the club on a permanent basis. In five seasons with the Prenton Park club, Nevin missed only a handful of games and continued to be selected by Scotland, winning 14 caps whilst with Rovers. Though not a prolific scorer, he netted a hat-trick in a 5-1 League Cup win over Oxford United in September 1993 and went on to score 39 goals in 239 games with a best of 16 in 54 games in 1992-93. The PFA Cairman was a great ambassador for Tranmere, leaving the club to play for Kilmarnock, whom he helped to fourth place in the Scottish Premier League in 1997-98.

NIXON, ERIC

Goalkeeper Eric Nixon joined Manchester City from Curzon Athletic for a fee of £1,000 in December 1983. With Alex Williams in such fine form, he had to wait until September 1985 before making his League debut in a 2-2 draw at home to West Ham United. Though he played in 28 games that season, he lost out to Perry Suckling in 1986-87 before regaining the number one spot the following season. During his time at Maine Road, Nixon became the first player to appear in all four divisions of the Football League in the same season after loan spells at Southampton, Bradford City, Wolves and Carlisle United.

When he joined Tranmere in March 1988 for a fee of £60,000, it was at the time a club record. He kept a clean sheet on his Rovers' debut as Carlisle United were beaten 3-0 at Prenton Park. Over the next seven seasons, Nixon missed very few games and was ever-present in 1989-90 and 1991-92. He helped the club win promotion in 1988-89 and 1990-91 when his outstanding display at Wembley helped Rovers beat Bolton 1-0 after extra-time in the Play-Off Final. After losing his place to Danny Coyne, Nixon failed to make an appearance for the club in 1995-96 but had loan spells at both Reading and Blackpool. He returned to Prenton Park to share the goalkeeping duties with Coyne in 1996-97 as well as going on loan to Bradford City. At the start of that season, he was appointed as the club's goalkeeping coach but in August 1997 after appearing in 440 first team games for the Prenton Park club, he left to join Stockport County for a fee of £100,000.

Eric Nixon, one of the club's greatest goalkeepers.

NOLAN, IAN

Energetic full-back Ian Nolan was on the books of Preston North End but after having failed to make much progress with the Deepdale club, left to play non-league football with Marine. After a series of impressive performances, Rovers paid £10,000 for his services in the summer of 1991. He made his debut for the club in a 1-1 draw at Wolverhampton Wanderers in October 1991 and went on to play in 40 games, winning the club's Player of the Year award. In 1992-93 he suffered a serious knee injury and missed most of the campaign. Despite regaining full fitness, he faced severe competition from Ged Brannan and Tony Thomas but went on to play in 53 games in 1993-94 as the club reached the play-offs for the second successive season.

Nolan had made 114 appearances for Tranmere when in August 1994 he joined Sheffield Wednesday for £1.5 million. Following his arrival at Hillsborough, he missed very few games and was called up to represent Northern Ireland in their World Cup qualifiers despite his Liverpool upbringing but in 1997-98 he suffered a badly broken leg when challenged by Spurs' Justin Edinburgh.

NON-LEAGUE

'Non-League' is the shorthand term for clubs which are not members of the Football League. Rovers have quite a good record against non-league opposition in the FA Cup and have only lost four matches.

Date	Opposition	FA Cup	Venue	Score
19.11.1921	Altrincham	4th Qual	Away	4-4
24.11.1921	Altrincham	4th Qual (R)	Home	2-4
18.11.1922	Wellington St. George	4th Qual	Away	0-2
17.11.1923	Ellesmere Port Town	4th Qual	Home	1-0
26.11.1927	Shirebrook	Round 1	Away	-1
28.11.1931	West Stanley	Round 1	Home	3-0
25.11.1933	Newark Town	Round 1	Home	7-0
24.11.1934	Stalybridge Celtic	Round 1	Home	3-1
14.12.1935	Scunthorpe Utd	Round 2	Home	6-2
29.11.1947	Stalybridge Celtic	Round 1	Home	2-0
25.11.1950	Cleator Moor Celtic	Round 1	Away	5-0

24.11.1951	Goole Town	Round 1	Home	4-2
15.12.1951	Blyth Spartans	Round 2	Home	1-1
19.12.1951	Blyth Spartans	Round 2 (1R)	Away	1-1*
03.01.1952	Blyth Spartans	Round 2 (1R)	Neutral	2-2**
07.01.1952	Blyth Spartans	Round 2 (2R)	Neutral	5-1***
22.11.1952	Ashington	Round 1	Home	8-1
19.11.1955	Easington Colliery	Round 1	Away	2-0
17.11.1956	Bishop Auckland	Round 1	Away	1-2
16.11.1957	Witton Albion	Round 1	Home	2-1
07.12.1957	Durham City	Round 2	Away	3-0
15.11.1958	Bishop Auckland	Round 1	Home	8-1
26.11.1966	Wigan Athletic	Round 1	Home	1-1
28.11.1966	Wigan Athletic	Round 1 (1R)	Away	1-0
18.11.1972	South Liverpool	Round 1	Away	2-0
23.11.1974	Farsley Celtic	Round 1	Away	2-0
22.11.1975	Coventry S.C.	Round 1	Away	0-2
25.11.1978	Boston United	Round 1	Home	2-1
24.11.1979	AP Leamington	Round 1	Home	9-0
20.11.1982	Scarborough	Round 1	Home	4-2
11.12.1982	Telford United	Round 2	Away	1-1
14.12.1982	Telford United	Round 2 (1R)	Home	2-1
17.11.1984	Bangor City	Round 1	Away	1-1
20.11.1984	Bangor City	Round 1 (1R)	Home	7-0
15.11.1986	Spennymoor Utd	Round 1	Away	3-2
10.12.1988	Northwich Victoria	Round 2	Away	2-1
17.11.1990	Halesowen Town	Round 1	Away	2-1
16.11.1991	Runcorn	Round 1	Away	3-0****
13.01.1998	Hereford United	Round 3	Away	3-0

* Abandoned

** At Brunton Park, Carlisle United

*** At Goodison Park, Everton

**** Switched to Prenton Park

O

O'BRIEN, LIAM

Republic of Ireland international Liam O'Brien won the first of his 16 caps whilst with Shamrock Rovers but in October 1986 he crossed the water to join Manchester United for a fee of £60,000. He made his league debut for the Old Trafford club two months later in a 2-0 home win over Leicester City. He went on to play in 36 games for United before joining Newcastle in November 1988 for £250,000.

The skilful playmaker stayed at St James Park for five seasons, scoring 22 goals in 185 first team games and helping the club win the First Division Championship, before signing for Tranmere Rovers for a fee of £300,000 in January 1994. After making his debut for Rovers in a 2-1 defeat at Bolton, O'Brien became an integral member of the Prenton Park club's side.

Liam O'Brien, who has won five caps for the Republic of Ireland since joining Tranmere Rovers.

Despite requiring surgery on a niggling injury, O'Brien fought his way back to become one of the club's most consistent and dependable players. Dangerous from set pieces, the Dublin-born midfielder has at the time of writing, scored 12 goals in 188 games for the Prenton Park club.

OLDEST PLAYER

The oldest player to line-up in a Tranmere Rovers team is John Aldridge. He was 39 years 227 days old when he played his last game for the club against Wolverhampton Wanderers (Home 2-1) on 3 May 1998.

OVERSEAS PLAYERS

The club's first overseas player was Nigerian Elkanah Onyeali who was studying at Birkenhead Technical College before scoring two goals on his debut in a 4-3 home win over Bournemouth in September 1960. He scored eight goals in 13 games before being released.

Italian international Ivano Bonetti who had played for Brescia, Atalanta, Sampdoria and Torino, joined Rovers from Grimsby Town in the summer of 1996. He appeared in 15 games before spending part of the season in Italy in an attempt to find a club there. He later returned to Prenton Park but was given a free transfer at the end of the 1996-97 season.

Dutch goalkeeper John Achterberg arrived at Prenton Park via the Bosman ruling, having previously played with FC Utrecht and PSV Eindhoven. Frenchman George Santos was also recruited via the Bosman agreement from FC Toulon. The 6ft 3ins defender was formerly with Olympic Marseilles and Valenciennes.

OWN GOALS

The first Tranmere Rovers player to put through his own goal in the Football League was Ernest Phillips who did so in the 4-1 defeat at Stalybridge Celtic on 2 September 1922.

The Tranmere player who has scored the most own goals during his time at Prenton Park is Ray Mathias who has put through his own net on seven occasions! He is closely followed by Ralph Millington and John King.

P

PALIOS, MARK

Mark Palios played his first game for Tranmere Rovers in a goalless draw at Aldershot on the opening day of the 1973-74 season. He went on to appear in 39 games during that campaign in which Rovers finished 16th in the Third Division. Over the next seven seasons, Palios was an established member of Rovers' first team and in 1975-76 helped the club win promotion from the Fourth Division. Though not a prolific scorer, he did net a hat-trick in a 5-0 home win over Chester in September 1977. In January 1980, Palios was allowed to leave Prenton Park and joined Crewe Alexandra.

Though the Railwaymen were bottom of the Fourth Division in 1981-82, Palios was the club's top scorer with 12 goals and went on to score 23 times in 118 games before rejoining Tranmere in March 1983.

He took his tally of goals to 33 in 286 League and Cup games in his two spells for Rovers before leaving to play non-league football for Bangor City.

PARNELL, ROY

Full-back Roy Parnell began his league career with Everton and made his debut for the Toffees in a 4-1 defeat at Wolverhampton Wanderers in January 1961. Finding it difficult to displace Alex Parker, Parnell, who had made just three league appearances in four seasons at Goodison Park, left to join Tranmere Rovers in the summer of 1964.

He played his first game for the Prenton Park club in a 5-2 home win over Halifax Town on the opening day of the 1964-65 season. He was one of only two ever-presents, goalkeeper Harry Leyland was the other, as Rovers finished the campaign fifth in Division Four. He missed just five games the following season as the club again finished in fifth place. In 1966-67 he was a member of Tranmere's promotion-winning side but in February 1967 after scoring three goals in 116 games he was transferred to Bury.

He gave the Shakers four seasons' service, appearing in 97 league games before hanging up his boots.

PARRY, LES

One of the quickest central defenders the club has ever had, Les Parry made his first team debut for Rovers in a 2-0 defeat at Brentford when he came on as a substitute for Alex Russell. After playing in three consecutive games during October 1972, Parry did not appear in the Tranmere side again for two years. After helping the club win promotion to the Third Division he became an established member of the Tranmere side and was ever-present in 1978-79.

During the early part of the 1982-83 season, Parry, who was an honest professional was sent-off twice in successive games as the referees clamped down on professional fouls. After serving his suspension, he returned to first team action only to break his leg in the 1-0 defeat at home to Hull City. Sadly the injury ended a career which had seen the dedicated Parry score four goals in 289 League and Cup games. He is now the Prenton Park club's physiotherapist.

PAYNE, GEORGE

Goalkeeper George Payne served with the RAF during the Second World War and played representative football for them. Having decided against taking up his love, Boxing, he signed professional forms for Tranmere Rovers in April 1947. Though he made his first team debut the following month in a 1-0 defeat at Hull City, his first few seasons at Prenton Park saw him sharing the goalkeeping duties with Harold Lloyd.

Payne played League football for Tranmere for 15 seasons, being an ever-present in 1955-56.

One of the greatest goalkeepers ever to play for the club, he played the last of his 467 League and Cup games in a 7-2 home win over Colchester United on 11 March 1961, when at the age of 39 years 202 days, he was the oldest player to appear in a league match for Rovers.

PENALTIES

When Tranmere Rovers beat Oldham Athletic 13-4 on Boxing Day 1935, Bunny Bell scored nine of the club's goals. He would have taken his tally of goals into double figures had he not missed a penalty!

PENALTY SHOOT-OUTS

Introduced as an alternative to the toss of a coin, the penalty shoot-out has been both kind and cruel to Rovers. In April 1988 the system cost the club a place in the Mercantile Centenary Final when they lost 1-0 to Nottingham Forest in the penalty shoot-out. When Rovers played Aston Villa in the League Cup semi-finals of 1993-94, the tie ended all-square at 4-4 over the two legs. Villa won the penalty shoot-out 5-4 to win through to the final against Manchester United. One penalty shoot-out that Tranmere did win was the 3-2 victory over Newcastle United in the League Cup competition of 1991-92 after the match in which John Aldridge scored a hat-trick had ended 6-6 after extra-time!

PEPLOW, STEVE

Liverpool-born Steve Peplow began his league career with his home-town club but after just two appearances for the Anfield club he joined Swindon Town. Though not a first team regular at the County Ground, he scored 11 goals in 40 league games before signing for Nottingham Forest. Unable to settle, he had a loan spell at

Mansfield Town before being transferred to Tranmere Rovers in January 1974, just six months after joining Forest.

After making his debut for Rovers in a 1-0 defeat at Port Vale, Peplow spent his first two seasons at Prenton Park in and out of the side before establishing himself as a first team regular in 1975-76. That season, he scored 11 goals in 50 games including a hat-trick in a 6-0 home win over Workington as Rovers won promotion to the Third Division. He went on to score 47 goals in 272 League and Cup appearances before hanging up his boots.

Steve Peplow, influential member of Rovers' promotion-winning side of 1975-76.

PHILPOTTS, DAVE

Dave Philpotts' playing career consisted of spells with Coventry City and Southport before he joined Tranmere Rovers in September 1974. He made his first team debut that month in a goalless home draw against West Ham United in a League Cup second round tie. The central defender became a regular member of the Rovers' first team and was ever-present in 1975-76 when the club won promotion to the Third Division.

He left Prenton Park to spend three and a half years playing in American football before returning for a second spell with Tranmere. He had taken his career record with the club to 12 goals in 237 League and Cup games when a back injury forced his retirement in 1984.

He was appointed Wigan Athletic coach in the summer of 1986 but later moved to assistant-manager before becoming manager in 1993.

Dave Philpotts

PITCH

The Prenton Park pitch measures 110 yards by 70 yards.

PLASTIC

There have been four Football League clubs that replaced their normal grass playing pitches with artificial surfaces at one stage or another. Queen's Park Rangers were the first in 1981, Luton Town, Oldham Athletic and Preston North End followed.

Tranmere Rovers have only played on North End's Deepdale plastic but in all three major competitions. They first played there in April 1987 when they lost 2-0 in a Fourth Division match. In 1988-89 an own goal by Atkins gave Rovers a 1-1 draw in an FA Cup first round tie, Ian Muir netting a hat-trick in a 3-0 replay win. In 1989-90, Rovers played on the Deepdale plastic in all three competitions, winning 4-3 in the League Cup, losing 1-0 in the FA Cup and drawing 2-2 in the League. The club last played on Preston's artificial surface in 1990-91, losing 1-0 in the Leyland DAF Cup Northern Area Final second leg but winning 4-0 in the League with Johnny Morrissey scoring two of the goals.

PLAY-OFFS

Tranmere Rovers have been involved in the divisional play-offs on five occasions.

In 1989-90, Rovers finished fourth in the Third Division and after beating Bury 2-0 on aggregate in the semi-finals, met Notts County in the final at Wembley but were beaten 2-0. The following season, Rovers finished fifth in Division Three and met Brentford in the semi-finals. Two goals from Steve Cooper gave them a 2-2 draw at Griffin Park, whilst a Ged Brannan goal separated the teams at Prenton Park. The final at Wembley against Bolton Wanderers was goalless until extra-time when Chris Malkin scored the game's only goal to send Rovers into the Second Division.

After one season, the Football League reorganised the game's structure and Rovers found themselves in the 'new' First Division. They finished fourth in 1992-93 but lost 5-4 on aggregate to Swindon Town in the play-off semi-final. In 1993-94 Rovers finished fifth in Division One to qualify for the play-offs but lost 2-1 over two legs to Leicester City. The club reached the play-offs for the third successive season in 1994-95 but after a disastrous 3-1 home defeat by Reading failed to make the Wembley final despite a fine rearguard action in a goalless draw at Elm Park.

POINTS

Under the three points for a win system which was introduced in 1981-82, Tranmere Rover's best points tally is 80 in seasons 1988-89 and 1989-90. In 1988-89 the club were runners-up in the Fourth Division and gained promotion to Division Three where they finished fourth and were beaten play-off semi-finalists the following season. However, the club's best points haul under the old two points for a win system was 60 in 1964-65 when they were fifth in Division Four. This would have netted them 87 points under the present system. Tranmere's worst record under either system was the meagre 17 points secured in 1938-39 when the club were relegated to the Third Division (North) after just one season in the Second Division.

POSTPONED

The bleak winter of 1962-63 – described at the time as the modern

ice-age – proved to be one of the most chaotic seasons in British soc-
cer history. The worst Saturday for league action in that awful winter
was 9 February when only seven Football League fixtures went ahead
and the entire Scottish League programme was frozen off. Rovers' FA
Cup game against Chelsea on 5 January was one of only three 32 third
round ties that went ahead. That game ended all-square at 2-2 though
Rovers lost the replay at Stamford Bridge 25 days later 3-1. In fact,
from 15 December 1962 to 27 February 1963, they were the only
games that Tranmere played!

On 29 September 1987, Tranmere's home game against Bolton
Wanderers was postponed because of a dispute over police manning
levels and costs. This led to the club being fined £2,000 and having
two points deducted.

PRENTON PARK

Though only yards away from their previous ground of the same
name, Rovers decided to keep the name Prenton Park and even had
their Main Stand moved on to the Borough Road side of their new
ground. A new stand housing 800 spectators was built on the oppo-
site side.

The ground was opened on 9 March 1912 by the Mayor of Birkenhead, George Proudman, for the Lancashire Combination match
against Lancaster Town. In 1913, the Bebington End was banked up
to form a Spion Kop and a year later, the club bought a structure com-
monly known as the Weekend Stand from the Oval Sports Ground at
Port Sunlight. This was divided into two and re-erected on either side
of the new Main Stand. In 1920 the Borough Road side of the ground
was fully covered but it was to be another 11 years or so before another change was made. This saw the terrace that backed onto
Prenton Road West covered by a roof with five pitched spans – immediately nicknamed the Cowshed!

During the Second World War, the cover on the Borough Road side
of the ground was destroyed during an air raid but was replaced once
the hostilities had ended. In 1958 the club installed floodlights, cour-
tesy of a £15,000 donation by the Supporters' Association and these
were first switched on for the visit of Rochdale in a Third Division
(North) game on 29 September 1958.

In 1967, Rovers replaced their Main Stand with a 4,000 seat stand that cost in the region of £80,000. This was opened by the then Sports Minister Denis Howell in December 1968. Four years later a crowd of 24,424 saw the FA Cup game against Stoke City to establish the club's record gate. In 1973 a strong gale almost blew the roof off the Cowshed and was replaced by a similar structure but with three spans instead of five. Over the coming years the ground began to deteriorate and the club who had to apply for re-election in 1981 came very close to extinction.

Bruce Osterman, a football-crazy US lawyer arrived at Prenton Park and though his intentions were good, he began to run up debts of over £500,000 and offered the site for a supermarket! Wirral Borough Council refused and in 1987, local millionaire Peter Johnson took over the running of the club.

Under the Safety of Sports Grounds Act in 1985, Prenton Park's capacity had been reduced to just 8,000. The Kop was closed completely and the Main Stand reduced to just 1,000 seats. However, under Johnson's leadership, the ground was soon transformed. New barriers and fences were installed and an electronic scoreboard was purchased from Goodison Park. In September 1988 a new set of floodlights costing £70,000 were switched on.

Despite the club's success on the field – rising from the Fourth to the Second Division and reaching the 'new' First Division play-offs – they fell behind schedule in their response to the Taylor Report for an all-seater stadium. In 1993 they decided to build three new sides to the ground at a total cost of £3.1 million. The work was completed within the space of just nine months, leaving Prenton Park with a total capacity of 16,789.

PRITCHARD, JOE

One of the club's greatest utility players, Joe Pritchard began his career as an amateur with Liverpool before moving to Prenton Park in September 1962. He made his debut in a goalless draw at Southport on 7 May 1963 and a week later scored twice in a 3-0 home win over Chester. His first three seasons with the club saw him make just 15 appearances before he established himself as a first team regular in 1965-66.

The following season he helped Rovers win promotion from the Fourth Division, scoring nine goals in 41 league games including one in a 3-0 win over Notts County on the final day of the season that helped clinch the fourth promotion spot. His best season in terms of goals scored was 1967-68 when as one of two ever-presents, he scored 11 league goals. Pritchard who went on to score 31 goals in 206 League and Cup games, wore eight different numbered outfield shirts for Rovers before leaving the club in 1970 to play non-league football for Ellesmere Port.

PROMOTION

Tranmere Rovers have been promoted on five occasions. They were first promoted in 1937-38 when they won the Third Division (North) Championship, finishing two points ahead of runners-up Doncaster Rovers. The club had come close to promotion earlier in the decade, twice finishing fourth and third in 1935-36. When Rovers were promoted for a second time in 1966-67, it was a similar story, for they had come close on two occasions prior to that. In 1964-65, Rovers were just one point behind Oxford United for the fourth promotion spot whilst the following season Colchester United beat the Prenton Park club on goal average after both clubs had totalled 56 points. When the club were eventually promoted in 1966-67, they ended the campaign in fourth place behind Barrow, Southport and champions Stockport County.

Rovers were promoted for a third time in 1975-76 when manager John King led the club back to the Third Division at the first attempt. Ronnie Moore scored 34 league goals including four goals in successive games as Stockport County (Home 5-0) and Newport County (Away 5-1) were beaten at the turn of the year. Rovers were promoted for a fourth time in 1988-89 when they ended the season as runners-up to Rotherham United.

The club were promoted for a fifth time in 1990-91 when after finishing the season in fifth place they qualified for the play-offs. After beating Brentford 3-2 over two legs, Rovers met Bolton Wanderers at Wembley. A goal in extra-time by Chris Malkin gave Rovers a 1-0 win and a place in the Second Division.

R

RECEIPTS

The club's record receipts are £130,541 fort he FA Cup fourth round tie against Sunderland at Prenton Park on 24 January 1998.

RE-ELECTION

Tranmere Rovers have had to apply for re-election to the Football League on three occasions – 1924-25 (21st in the Third Division North) 1956-57 (23rd in the Third Division North) and 1980-81 (21st in the Fourth Division).

RELEGATION

Tranmere Rovers have been relegated on four occasions. After winning the Third Division (North) Championship in 1937-38, Rovers were relegated after just one season of Second Division football. It was a disastrous season with the club winning just six of its 42 games and conceding 99 goals. The club's second experience of relegation occurred in 1960-61 after they had won a place in the new Third Division three seasons earlier. The club conceded 115 goals and suffered a number of heavy defeats at Queen's Park Rangers (Lost 9-2) and at home to Bury (Lost 7-1) and Grimsby Town (Lost 6-3). Rovers were relegated for a third time in 1974-75 after finishing 22nd in the Third Division. However, the club did turn in some good performances, none more so than the 6-1 home win over Hereford United. It was s taste of things to come, for the following season, Rovers won promotion from the Fourth Division at the first time of asking.

The club's last experience of relegation was in 1978-79 when they won just six of their 46 matches in the Third Division – the lowest number of league wins in the club's history. Rovers also only scored 45 goals and failed to find the net in 16 of their matches.

RIDDING, BILL

Bill Ridding began his Football League career with Tranmere Rovers, making his debut in a 1-0 home win over Bradford City in September 1928. The following season he scored 12 goals in 15 games including a hat-trick in a 7-1 defeat of Hartlepool United and four goals in the 5-2 win over Barrow. This form attracted the attention of a number of top clubs and in March 1930 he joined Manchester City. From Maine Road, he moved across the city to Old Trafford and then to Northampton. He had another brief spell with Tranmere before joining Oldham Athletic where a double cartilage injury forced his retirement.

He returned to Prenton Park as the 'A' team trainer and was appointed trainer after the death of Jimmy Moreton. He also managed the club from 1939 to 1945 despite being officially titled the club's trainer and even incorporated other jobs such as secretary, kit washer and groundsman!

Bill Ridding, who played for both Manchester clubs after Prenton Park.

In 1946 he joined Bolton Wanderers as trainer and four years later he was appointed by the FA as England's trainer for the World Cup in Brazil.

In February 1951 he was appointed secretary-manager of Bolton Wanderers, also acting as the club's trainer for a while. In 1953 he led the Wanderers to Wembley where they lost 4-3 to Blackpool but five years later they returned to win the FA Cup after beating Manchester United 2-0 in the final. He left Burnden Park in 1968 to concentrate on his physiotherapy business, later joining Lancashire County Cricket Club in that capacity. Dying at the age of 70 in September 1981, he was at the time of his departure, second only to Matt Busby as the League's longest-serving manager.

ROBERTSON, EDDIE

Eddie Robertson played his early football with Linithgow Rose in his native Scotland before coming south of the border to play league football for Bury. In seven seasons in the Gigg Lane club's first team, Robertson appeared in over 200 League and Cup games and helped the Shakers win the Third Division Championship in 1960-61.

In October 1963 he joined Wrexham but after the Welsh club were relegated he moved to Prenton Park in the summer of 1964 after being signed by Dave Russell. He made his Rovers' debut in a 2-1 defeat at Darlington in September 1964 and over the next few seasons missed very few matches. In 1966-67 he helped the club win promotion from the Fourth Division and scored his only goal for Rovers in a 2-1 home win over Port Vale.

Robertson, who appeared in 161 games for Rovers bought a newsagent's shop after leaving the game but returned to Prenton Park as coach in 1975 following the appointment of Johnny King. After helping the club win promotion to the Third Division in 1975-76, this much respected and popular coach was appointed assistant-manager. Sadly in December 1981, he collapsed and died on West Kirby beach during a training session – he was just 46. A great servant to Tranmere Rovers, his name lives on in the form of a Supporters' Association Trophy for the 'Players' Player'.

ROSENTHAL, ABE

Liverpool-born forward Abe Rosenthal played in just one league game for Rovers prior to the outbreak of the Second World War, appearing for the club in a 2-1 defeat at Millwall on the final day of the 1938-39 season when the club were already relegated. After 'guesting' for a number of clubs during the war years, he returned to Prenton Park for the 1946-47 season but then left to join Bradford City. Rosenthal's league career was divided between Rovers and the Valley Parade club, having three spells with each team.. His most productive season for Tranmere was 1950-51 when his total of 18 goals in 36 games included four in a 7-2 home win over York City on the opening day of the season.

Rosenthal, who had an ice cream business in Bradford was a flamboyant character and played the last of his 130 games in which he scored 44 goals in March 1955. Sadly, he died in 1986 after chasing an intruder at his home.

ROWLANDS, STAN

Born near Welshpool, Stan Rowlands played his early football for Birkenhead North End but was soon transferred to Nottingham Forest. After just one season at the City Ground, he had a brief spell with South Liverpool before joining Wrexham. In his only season at the Racecourse Ground prior to the First World War, Rowlands was the club's top scorer with 18 goals in 30 games including a hat-trick in a 3-1 win over Walsall.

He joined Tranmere Rovers in 1913 and the following season, his 32 goals helped the club win the Lancashire Combination title. His goalscoring exploits led to him becoming the club's first player to win international recognition when he played in Wales' 2-0 defeat against England at Ninian Park. After leaving Prenton Park he had spells with Reading, Crewe Alexandra and Wrexham again before ending his career with Oswestry.

ROWLEY, TONY

Born in Porthcawl, Tony Rowley was originally on Birmingham City's books but failed to make any league appearances and was transferred to non-league Stourbridge. Liverpool picked him up in October 1953 and he scored a hat-trick on his debut. His tally of 38 goals in 60 appearances over four seasons at Anfield is quite impressive but Rowley had his critics. There were some who said he was too slow and consequently he drifted in and out of the Liverpool team.

Tranmere manager Peter Farrell paid a club record fee of £3,500 for his services in March 1958. He made his debut in Rovers' colours in a 2-0 home win over Halifax Town and ended the season with just one goal in nine games. However, in 1958-59 he was the club's joint-top scorer with Keith Williams, both players netting 26 goals. Included in Tony Rowley's total was four goals in a 9-0 home win over Accrington Stanley and a spell where he scored eight goals in six consecutive games. His form that season led to him being capped by Wales against Northern Ireland in Belfast, a match the Welsh lost 4-1.

In 1959-60, Rowley was the club's leading scorer with 14 goals but at the end of the following season, after which he had scored 49 goals in 108 games, he left Prenton Park to play non-league football for Bangor City.

RUSSELL, DAVE

Dundee-born Dave Russell began his career with his home-town club before moving to East Fife whom he helped to win the Scottish Cup Final in 1938. In the close season he joined Sheffield Wednesday and was ever-present in the Owls' side as they finished third in Division Two in 1938-39. During the war he joined the RAF thus limiting his footballing activities and when the hostilities ended, he became coach to the Danish FA.

In 1950 he returned to these shores to become Bury's coach, later taking over the position of secretary-manager. During his first few years in charge, the Gigg Lane club had a constant struggle against relegation and were eventually relegated in 1957 after 63 years of membership in the top two divisions. He had just led the Shakers to the Third Division Championship in 1960-61 when he left to become manager of Tranmere Rovers, who were two divisions lower than Bury!

At Prenton Park he had five seasons of frustration before leading the club to promotion in 1966-67. He stepped down as team manager in 1969, letting his right-hand man Jackie Wright take over. Russell became the club's general manager, a position he held until 1978.

S

SECOND DIVISION

Tranmere Rovers have had two spells in the Second Division, each lasting just one season. The club's first spell followed their promotion as champions of the Third Division (North) in 1937-38. The campaign was a great disappointment, Rovers finished bottom of the Second Division with just 17 points and suffered some heavy defeats, notably the 9-3 win for Manchester City at Prenton Park on Boxing Day, who then followed it up with a 5-2 win at Maine Road the following day!

The club's second spell in Division Two came in 1991-92 following their promotion the previous season. This time Rovers finished 14th but moved up to the 'new' First Division for the 1992-93 season following reorganisation by the Football League.

SHERPA VAN TROPHY

The competition for Associate Members of the Football League was first sponsored for the 1987-88 season by Sherpa Van. Tranmere's first match in the Sherpa Van Trophy competition saw them play out a goalless draw at Rochdale but then they lost 2-1 at home to Burnley and so failed to qualify for the knockout stages.

In 1988-89, goals from Steel and Mungall gave them a 2-1 home win over Stockport County, whilst the club's top goalscorer Ian Muir scored the goal that enabled them to draw 1-1 at Crewe Alexandra. In the first round, Rovers went down 1-0 at home to Wigan Athletic in front of a Prenton Park crowd of 2,997.

SINCLAIR, ROY

Roy Sinclair was an amateur on Liverpool's books when he joined Tranmere Rovers in October 1963 and though he impressed in the club's reserve side, he had to wait until the last game of the 1963-64 season before making his debut in a 2-0 win at Oxford United.

Over the next five seasons, Sinclair created a number of goalscoring chances for the likes of Dyson, McDonnell and Manning but did manage to score a hat-trick himself during the club's 6-2 home win over Rochdale in December 1965. In March 1969, Sinclair left Prenton Park to play for Watford but after a loan spell at Chester he returned to play for Rovers a second time in the summer of 1972. He stayed for just one season, taking his tally of goals to 18 in 166 games in his two spells with the club.

SPENCER, REG

Left-half Reg Spencer joined Tranmere Rovers from local football in 1931 and made his first team debut in a 3-3 draw at Gateshead in February 1932. Gateshead were also Rovers' opponents when Spencer scored the first of his three goals for the club in a 4-2 home win eight months later. Over the next six seasons, Spencer missed very few matches, going on to appear in 256 games for the Prenton Park club.

Strong in the tackle and a good distributor of the ball, his performances during the 1937-38 season were instrumental in the club winning the Third Division (North) Championship as they finished two points ahead of runners-up Doncaster Rovers.

The following season, Spencer was replaced by Alf Day who had joined the club from Southampton and only appeared in two league games. In a season in which the club were relegated after just one season of Second Division football, Spencer's vast experience was sorely missed.

SPONSORS

The club's official sponsors are Wirral Borough Council. Previous sponsors have included Storeton Motors, Cathedral Tours, Stairways and Hugh Fowlerton Cutlery of Heswall.

STEEL, JIM

Dumfries-born Jim Steel began his league career with Oldham Athletic where he scored 24 goals in 108 games before loan spells at Wigan and Wrexham. During his stay at the Racecourse Ground, he scored six goals in nine outings and though the Welsh club wanted to sign him, they were having financial difficulties and couldn't afford the £10,000 fee. Steel joined Port Vale and helped the Valiants win promotion to the Third Division but midway through the 1983-84 season, he left Vale Park to join Wrexham.

He was the club's leading scorer in 1984-85 with 14 league goals. He scored a similar total the following season and netted seven goals in the club's successful Welsh Cup campaign. He headed the Robins' scoring charts again in 1986-87 with 17 league goals and netted his first league hat-trick in a 4-3 win over Peterborough United. His performances for the Robins led to FC Porto trying to sign him but when the deal failed to materialise, he went on loan to Spanish side Real Coruna. Steel, who had scored 72 goals in 230 games for Wrexham later joined Tranmere Rovers.

He made his debut in a 2-1 win at Hartlepool United on 21 November 1987 and scored his first goal for the club later that month in a 4-0 home win over Newport County. He helped the Prenton Park club win promotion from the Fourth Division in 1988-89 and then in 1989-90 after the club had finished fourth in the Third Division, was outstanding in the play-offs where Tranmere lost to Notts County at Wembley. Also that season he scored one of Rovers' goals in a 2-1 win over Bristol Rovers also at Wembley as the Prenton Park club won the Leyland DAF Trophy. In 1990-91, Rovers eventually won promotion to the Second Division, beating Bolton Wanderers 1-0 after extra-time in the play-off final at Wembley. However, at the end of the following season, Steel, who had scored 47 goals in 226 games for Tranmere, left the game to join the Merseyside police force.

Jim Steel, scorer of one of Tranmere's goals in the Leyland DAF Cup Final.

STEELE, PERCY

Percy Steele began his career with Everton for whom he signed amateur forms before arriving at Prenton Park during the Second World War. After having turned professional in January 1944, he played in a number of wartime games before making his Football League debut in a 2-1 defeat at Accrington Stanley in December 1946.

One of the club's greatest utility players, he appeared at full-back, half-back, inside-forward or on either wing, though he was mainly regarded as a right-back. Although he was never ever-present, Steele missed very few games over the ten seasons he spent with the club, appearing in 338 League and Cup games.

His only goal for the club came in a Liverpool Senior Cup tie in March 1948 when Rovers beat New Brighton 3-0. Steele left Prenton Park in 1956 and joined non-league Burscough after which he hung up his boots.

STEVENS, GARY

Joining Everton straight from school, Gary Stevens made such an impact in the club's Central League side that he was given his first team debut in a 1-1 draw at West Ham United in October 1981. However, it was another 12 months before he gained a regular place in the Everton side, replacing Brian Borrows. His great composure on the ball, allied to his natural sprinting ability led to his call-up to the full England squad for the World Cup qualifier against Northern Ireland in February 1985, although it was later that year when he made his full debut against World Cup holders Italy in Mexico. A member of the England team which reached the 1986 World Cup quarter-finals, he went on to appear in 46 games for his country. For Everton, he won two League Championship medals, an FA Cup winners' medal and a European Cup Winners' Cup medal. After appearing in 284 League and Cup games, he left Goodison in the 1988 close season to sign for Glasgow Rangers for a fee of £1.25 million. At Ibrox he won six Scottish Premier Division Championship medals, a Scottish Cup winners' medal and three Scottish League Cup medals. In September 1994 after appearing in 245 first team games for the Scottish giants, he returned to Merseyside to play for Tranmere Rovers, costing the Prenton Park club £350,000.

He made his debut in a 1-0 home win over Sunderland and later that season scored the first of his two goals for the club in a 2-2 draw at Swindon Town. His versatility and experience proved an invaluable asset in his four seasons at Prenton Park where apart from a spell when he suffered a badly broken forearm, he missed very few games. He had appeared in 150 League and Cup games for Rovers when in the summer of 1998 he was released by the club on a free transfer.

STORTON, STAN

Stan Storton, older brother of Trevor was on Huddersfield Town's books as an amateur before moving to Bradford City where he began his league career. He appeared in 111 games for the Valley Parade club before following a brief spell with Darlington he joined Hartlepool United. The strong-tackling full-back had played in 72 league games for 'The Pool' when he was transferred to Tranmere in the summer of 1966.

He made his debut for Rovers on 10 September 1966 against his former club Hartlepool United and was outstanding in a 2-0 win for the Prenton Park side. Over the next four seasons, Stan Storton missed very few games and though he only scored two goals in that time, they were both spectacular strikes. He had played in 139 games for the club when he left Prenton Park at the end of the 1969-70 season. Stan Storton later became one of the most respected of non-league managers in the game when he took charge of Telford United.

STORTON, TREVOR

Trevor Storton who was 10 years younger than Stan, joined Rovers straight from school on the recommendation of his older brother. He played his first game for the club in a 3-2 home win over Swindon Town in November 1967, a match in which George Yardley scored all Rovers' goals. He established himself in the Tranmere side in 1968-69 and was a first team regular at Prenton Park for five seasons. Able to play in midfield or the centre of defence, he went on to score 10 goals in 135 games with nine of them coming in his last season with the club.

In August 1972 he joined Liverpool for a fee of £25,000 but in two seasons at Anfield, only appeared in 12 League and Cup games before

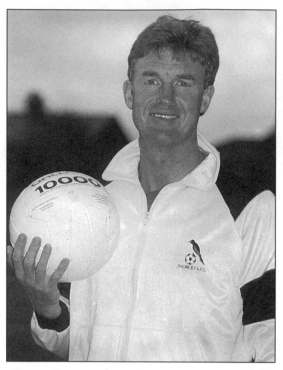

Trevor Storton, who spent two seasons at Anfield after leaving Tranmere.

being allowed to join Chester City. He went on to give the Cestrians great service, appearing in 396 League games in 10 seasons with the club before trying his hand at management with Oswestry and Chorley.

STUART, TOM

Left-back Tom Stuart joined Rovers from Bootle Albion and made his debut in the club's first-ever Football League game when they beat Crewe Alexandra 4-1 at Prenton Park. In fact, the defender scored one of the club's goals in the victory over the Gresty Road club. He missed very few games over the next five seasons, being ever-present in 1922-23 and 1923-24 and appearing in 113 consecutive league games. Two seasons later, Stuart switched to right-back to accommodate Percy Thirkell.

After missing the entire 1926-27 campaign through injury and a loss of form, Stuart played the last of his 205 games in which he scored 13 goals against Rotherham United in January 1928, playing at centre-half in place of the injured Jack Bamber.

SUBSTITUTES

Substitutes were first allowed in the Football League in the 1965-66 season. The first appearance of a substitute in league football came at Burnden Park when Charlton Athletic's Keith Peacock came on during Bolton's 4-2 win. Tranmere Rover's first substitute was Jack

Lornie who came on for Mandy Hill in the club's second game of the season on 23 August 1965, a 1-0 win over Chester.

The first goalscoring number twelve was former Bolton Wanderers' player Graham Stanley. In what was his only appearance for the club, he replaced Barry Dyson and scored Rovers' third goal in a 3-1 win at Aldershot.

Under the single substitute rule, the greatest number of substitutes used by Tranmere in a single season was 35 in 1983-84 but, in 1986-87, two substitutes were allowed and, in 1990-91, the club used 59. In recent years, the Football League have allowed three substitutes and in 1996-97, 108 were used.

The greatest number of substitute appearances for Tranmere in the Football League has been made by Johnny Morrissey who has, at the time of writing, come on during 55 league games. Taking into consideration all games, Chris Malkin holds the record with 64 appearances as a substitute. Malkin is one of three players, the others being Eddie Bishop and Alan Mahon who hold the club record with an extraordinary 15 league appearances as a substitute during a season.

SUNDAY FOOTBALL

The first-ever Sunday matches in the Football League took place on 20 January 1974 as a result of the three-day week imposed by the government during its trial of strength with the coalminers. On that day, Rovers entertained Aldershot but went down 1-0 in front of a Prenton Park crowd of 4,908. This was well up on the club's previous home crowd of 2,766 for the visit of Rochdale on 29 December 1973.

SUSTAINED SCORING

In 1933-34, Bunny Bell set a new club record when he scored 40 goals in 38 League and Cup games for Rovers. He scored four goals on two occasions as Barnsley (Home 5-2) and Newark Town (Home 7-0) were beaten and netted hat-tricks against Chester (Home 6-1) Crewe Alexandra (Home 5-1) York City (Home 3-0) and Halifax Town (Home 3-2).

T

THIRD DIVISION

Tranmere Rovers have had five spells in the Third Division. Their first began with the club's initial season in the Football League in 1921-22 and lasted for 17 seasons. During that time, the club had to apply for re-election in 1924-25 and had a best finish of third in 1935-36 before winning the Third Division (North) Championship in 1937-38. That season the club finished two points ahead of Doncaster Rovers with whom they drew 1-1 in the final game of the season. The club were relegated after just one season in the Second Division and when League football resumed in 1946-47, Rovers began their second spell in Division Three. It was to last 15 seasons and saw them apply for re-election again in 1956-57 before a Fourth Division was formed in 1958-59. Rovers finished 21st in 1960-61 and were relegated. The club's third spell began in 1967-68 and lasted eight seasons before relegation in 1974-75. Rovers' fourth spell began two seasons later after the club had won promotion from the Fourth Division at the first attempt. This time they spent three seasons in the Third Division before another relegation in 1978-79. The club's fifth and final session in the Third Division began in 1989-90 but lasted just two seasons for in 1990-91 they won promotion to the Second Division after beating Bolton Wanderers 1-0 in the play-off final at Wembley.

THIRKELL, PERCY

Left-back Percy Thirkell began his Football League career with Bolton Wanderers and made 15 first team appearances for the Trotters during their FA Cup winning season of 1922-23. He joined Tranmere in the summer of 1925 and made his debut for the Prenton Park club in a 2-1 home win over Durham on the opening day of the 1925-26 season. He was one of three ever-presents that season and after playing in all of the club's games again in 1926-27 went on to appear in 98 consecutive League and Cup games following his debut.

Thirkell was a regular member of the Rovers' defence for five seasons, appearing in 184 games for the club before being allowed to leave and join Congleton.

THOMAS, TONY

The strong-running right-back made his debut for Rovers in a 1-1 draw at Peterborough United in February 1989, when at the age of 17 he came on as a substitute for Mark Hughes. He won a Leyland DAF Cup winners' medal in 1990 as Rovers beat Bristol Rovers 2-1 in the Wembley final and the following year played his part in the club's promotion to the Second Division via the play-offs. He went on to be a virtual ever-present until the end of the 1996-97 season, having scored 14 goals in 314 games.

'Thomas the Tank' as he is affectionately known, was on the transfer list for much of his last couple of seasons at Prenton Park, playing on a week-to-week contract. He eventually left the club in August 1997, joining Everton for a fee of £400,000. He was delighted by the switch, having supported Everton as a child, but his progress at Goodison has been hampered by a number of injuries.

Tony Thomas displaying his shooting power.

THOMPSON, ANDY

Determined little full-back Andy Thompson began his career with West Bromwich Albion but was never given a chance at the Hawthorns and in November 1986 he joined Wolverhampton Wanderers along with Steve Bull.

In his first full season with the club he helped Wolves win the Fourth Division Championship and the Sherpa Van Trophy, appearing in 56 first team games. He was the only ever-present in 1988-89 as Wolves won the Third Division title and missed very few games over the next eight seasons.

Thompson had scored 45 goals in 451 first team games for Wolves before leaving Molineux in July 1997 to join Tranmere Rovers on a free transfer. He made his debut at his first club, Rovers losing 2-1 to West Bromwich Albion. That season he missed just two games as Rovers ended the campaign in 14th place in the First Division. He has now played in almost 100 games for the Prenton Park club.

TRANSFERS

The club's record transfer fee received is the £2 million that Nottingham Forest paid for Alan Rogers in July 1997. Tranmere's record transfer fee paid is £450,000 to Aston Villa for the services of Shaun Teale in August 1995.

TWINS

David Jackson and his brother Peter are the only set of twins to have played league football for Tranmere Rovers.

Peter Jackson is ten seconds older than his twin brother David. The Jacksons' careers practically ran parallel with each other and their appearances for three league and three non-league clubs is unique. Peter Jackson made his league debut alongside his brother, playing for Wrexham against Carlisle United in October 1954. When their father, who was the Wrexham manager left to join Bradford City, they saw the season out with Marine before joining Jackson senior at Valley Parade. When their father left City, the twins joined Tranmere Rovers. David left to play for Halifax and in the 1965 close season, Peter left Prenton Park to team up with David, who had moved to Frickley Colliery. They later played together at Altrincham and Hyde United, with Peter having spells at Macclesfield and Guiseley.

TYNAN, BOBBY

An England Youth international, Bobby Tynan was playing for Liverpool's Central League side when Ron Yeats brought him to Prenton Park towards the end of the 1972-73 season. He made his debut in a 2-2 draw at Blackburn Rovers in March 1973 and though he failed to find the net, he impressed in the six games he played in that campaign. For the next five seasons, Tynan was a virtual ever-present, playing just behind Rovers' front two of John James and Ronnie Moore. Although he was more of a goal maker, he did score 31 goals in his 221 League and Cup games including a hat-trick in a 3-1 home win over Sheffield Wednesday on Boxing Day 1977.

Throughout his stay at Prenton Park, Tynan was the subject of big money offers from a number of top flight clubs. Rovers managed to hold out until the summer of 1978 when they accepted an £100,000 bid from Blackpool.

Sadly he sustained a bad knee injury during the club's pre-season tour and never kicked a ball in league football for the Seasiders.

VEITCH, TOMMY

Midfielder Tommy Veitch played his early football with Hearts but after failing to win a regular place in the Tynecastle club's side, he joined Tranmere Rovers on a free transfer in the summer of 1972.

The strong-tackling Veitch went straight into Ron Yeats' side and made his debut in a 1-0 defeat at Watford on the opening day of the 1972-73 season. More of a creator of goals than a goalscorer, he only found the net five times in 90 first team appearances for the Prenton Park club but whenever he did, Rovers never lost!

He was released at the end of the 1974-75 campaign after a season with Halifax Town where he made 22 league appearances, he ended his league career with Hartlepool United. He returned to his native

Edinburgh but in 1985 he became very ill and died at the tragically young age of 38.

VICKERS, STEVE

Bishop Auckland-born defender Steve Vickers joined Tranmere Rovers from Spennymoor in 1985 after turning down Middlesborough, the club he left Rovers for in 1993. Vickers made his debut for Tranmere in a 3-1 home defeat by Northampton Town in April 1986, establishing himself as the club's first-choice centre-half the following season. Vickers, who was ever-present in seasons 1987-88 and 1988-89, appeared in 148 consecutive games for Rovers during this period and missed very few games in eight seasons at Prenton Park.

He won a Leyland DAF Cup winners' medal in 1989 and made 387 League and Cup appearances as the Wirral club rose from the old Fourth Division to become perennial play-off candidates in Division One.

Vickers eventually left Prenton Park in December 1993, joining Middlesborough for £700,000. He was a vital member of the team that won promotion to the top flight in Bryan Robson's first season at the club and once in the Premier League won admiration for his intelligent defending.

VICTORIES IN A SEASON – HIGHEST

In the 1964-65 season, Tranmere Rovers won 27 of their 46 league fixtures in finishing fifth in Division Four.

VICTORIES IN A SEASON – LOWEST

Tranmere's poorest performance was in seasons 1938-39 and 1978-79 when they won only six matches out of their 42 and 46 games respectively. Not surprisingly the club finished bottom of the Second Division in 1938-39 and 23rd in the Third Division in 1978-79, being relegated on both occasions.

Steve Vickers, a virtual ever-present during his stay at Prenton Park.

WARING, TOM 'PONGO'

Birkenhead-born Tom 'Pongo' Waring played for his school team and Birkenhead Boys before signing for Tranmere Celtic in 1921 and joining Tranmere Rovers as a professional in January 1926.

He made his debut in a 2-1 defeat at Rotherham United in the second game of the 1927-28 season, a campaign in which he scored 24 goals in 27 games. Included in that total were a hat-trick in a 5-2 home win over Wigan Borough and six goals as Rovers blasted Durham City 11-1 in the FA Cup. It was this kind of form that attracted the League's top clubs and though Arsenal, Bolton and Manchester United had shown an interest in young Waring, it was Aston Villa who secured his services for £4,700.

When he made his debut for Villa in a Central League fixture against rivals Birmingham, a crowd of 23,000 turned out to see him. They were not disappointed as he hit a hat-trick in Villa's victory. When he did play for the first team against Sunderland at Roker Park, he scored in Villa's 3-2 win. The following season he hit the first of ten hat-tricks in Villa's colours as Arsenal were beaten 5-2 at Highbury. In 1930-31 Pongo Waring created a club record by scoring 50 goals, 49 of them in the First Division. He scored 13 goals in the firsts even games of the season, including all four on the opening day when Villa beat Manchester United 4-3. He also scored four in a 6-1 win over West Ham United and all four in a 4-2 win over Sunderland. In November 1935, after scoring 167 goals in 226 League and Cup games, he was surprisingly allowed to join Barnsley. A crowd of over 5,000 showed their disapproval of the move by calling for his return. However, Waring was at Oakwell for less than a year before moving to Wolves and then returning to Tranmere Rovers.

He spent two seasons at Prenton Park and was top scorer in each with a best of 23 in 1937-38 when Rovers won the Third Division (North) Championship. He had scored 67 goals in 105 games in his two spells with the club before leaving to play for Accrington Stanley and later Bath City. He ended his playing days 'guesting' for New Brighton during the war.

WARTIME FOOTBALL

Despite the outbreak of war in 1914, the football leagues embarked upon their planned programme of matches for the ensuing season and these were completed on schedule at the end of April the following year. Rovers who had won the Lancashire Combination in 1913-14 continued as one of the best teams in the competition and also produced their highest score in the FA Cup with a 13-0 defeat of Oswestry United. During the First World War, Rovers played as many matches as they could in the leagues organised by the Lancashire Combination.

In contrast to the events of 1914, once war was declared on 3 September 1939, the Football League programme of 1939-40 was immediately suspended and the government forbade any major sporting event, so that for a while there was no football of any description.

Eventually registered leagues were formed and in 1939-40, Rovers played in the West League but without much success. The following season, the competition was reorganised and Tranmere took part in the North League, though over the next five seasons there were times when manager Bill Ridding found it difficult to raise a team. In 1945, wartime football was once more reorganised and Rovers played in the Third Division north-west region. The war years did see Rovers suffered their heaviest defeat when on 28 February 1942, Blackpool beat the Prenton Park club 15-3. In that match the Seasiders' Jock Dodds scored seven goals including a hat-trick in the space of two-and-a-half minutes.

WATTS, FAREWELL

Signed from Newport County, inside-forward Farewell Watts made his debut for Rovers in a 2-1 home defeat by Chesterfield on 22 April 1930, scoring his first goal for the club in the final game of the season four days later as Rovers lost 5-1 at home to Port Vale. The following season, Watts formed a prolific goalscoring partnership with Ernie Dixon and in a campaign in which he was one of four ever-presents, he scored 29 goals in 44 games including a hat-trick in a 5-4 home win over Hartlepool United. On Christmas Day 1931, Watts scored five goals in a 9-1 demolition of Rochdale in front of a Prenton Park crowd of 5,719. In both of those seasons, Rovers finished fourth in the Third Division (North), Watts scoring 41 goals in 67 league games as the club came close to promotion in each campaign. He had scored 60 goals in 128 games for Rovers when, at the end of the 1933-34 season, he left the club.

WEB SITE

The official internet World Wide Web site is at:

www.merseyworld.com/rovers/

WELSH CUP

The Welsh Cup is the third oldest cup competition in the world and was instituted in 1877 with the first final being played at Acton Park, Wrexham on 30 March 1878 when Wrexham beat Druids 1-0.

Tranmere first entered the Welsh Cup in 1906-07 and again the following two seasons but with little success. It was 1932-33 before the club re-entered the competition, losing 4-2 to Cardiff City at Ninian Park. The following season Rovers made it all the way to the final but lost 3-0 in a replay against Bristol City after the first match had been drawn. Rovers reached the final again in 1934-35, beating Flint Town (Away 5-0) Lovells Athletic (Away 6-5 after a 1-1 draw) and Shrewsbury Town (Away 3-0). In the final at Sealand Road, a goal from Billy Woodward gave Rovers a 1-0 victory.

WHEELER, JOHNNY

Johnny Wheeler joined Tranmere Rovers from Carlton and after making his debut in a 2-1 home defeat at the hands of Hull City on the opening day of the 1948-49 season, went on to score 11 goals in 106 games for the Prenton Park club before becoming Bolton manager Bill Ridding's first signing when he joined the Wanderers in February 1951. He played his first game for the then Burnden Park club in a 2-1 home win over Liverpool and then held his place virtually unchallenged for the next five seasons.

On 3 January 1953 he was asked to play as an emergency centre-forward and responded with a hat-trick in a 4-0 win over Blackpool. After appearing in that season's FA Cup Final and winning Football League and England 'B' honours, he won his only full cap for his country when in October 1954 he played against Northern Ireland in Belfast. He went on to score 18 goals in 205 games for

Bolton before being released to join his cousin Ronnie Moran at Liverpool.

However, by the time he arrived at Anfield, his best days were over, though he was still a useful servant to the club, playing in 177 games and scoring 23 goals. By the time the Reds finally escaped the lower divisions, his days were over and he made just one appearance during the club's Second Division Championship winning season of 1961-62. The following season he left the club to become assistant-trainer at Bury.

WHITEHURST, BERT

One of the game's most prolific goalscorer, there is no doubt that Bradford City's Third Division (North) Championship winning season of 1928-29 belongs to Bert Whitehurst. Signed from Liverpool in February 1929, he scored 24 goals in 15 appearances including two in City's 4-3 win at Lincoln City on his debut. He scored a club record seven goals in the 8-0 win over Tranmere Rovers and four more three days later in an 8-0 victory against Barrow. Whenever Whitehurst was in the side that season, City did not lose a game, winning 13 and drawing two of the games.

Two seasons later he was transferred to Tranmere Rovers and made his debut in a 1-0 defeat at Southport in September 1931. In only his fifth game for the club and his first at centre-forward, he scored four goals in an 8-1 home win over Accrington Stanley. In 1932-33 he was the club's joint-top scorer with Bunny Bell with 17 goals but in 1934 after taking his tally of goals to 35 in 90 games, Whitehurst tragically collapsed and died after a training session at Prenton Park.

WILLIAMS, GARY

Nantwich-born utility player Gary Williams joined the club as a non-contract player in 1976 and made his debut in a 3-0 defeat at Gillingham in May 1977, the club's last game of the season. He then left Prenton Park to try his luck abroad with Swedish club Djurgardens before returning to Football League action with Blackpool in the summer of 1980. After just one season at Bloomfield Road which saw the Seasiders relegated to the Fourth Division, he left to play for Swindon Town before rejoining Tranmere in February 1983.

In his second spell with Rovers, he showed his versatility by wearing seven different numbered outfield shirts and was at home in both midfield and at full-back. He missed very few matches in the seven seasons he was at Prenton Park and in 1988-89, his last campaign with the club, he helped Rovers win promotion to the Third Division. Williams, who scored 18 goals in 204 games left the first-class game at the end of that season.

WILLIAMS, JOHN

Tall central defender John Williams began his league career with Tranmere Rovers, making his debut in a 4-1 defeat at Swindon Town in March 1979. Over the next two seasons, Williams made just four appearances but in 1980-81 he established himself in the heart of the Rovers' defence and over the next five seasons, missed only a handful of games. He went on to score 13 goals in 201 League and Cup games before leaving Prenton Park to join Port Vale for £12,000 in July 1985.

In his first season at Vale Park he helped the club win promotion to the Third Division but after losing form the following campaign, was allowed to join Bournemouth. After a loan spell with Wigan Athletic, he ended his league career with Cardiff City. Williams later returned to Bournemouth as the community development officer before becoming their assistant-manager.

WILLIAMS, KEITH

A former Everton junior, he did not get a league chance with the Goodison Park club and in May 1957 he joined his older brother Ray at Prenton Park.

He made his debut for Rovers in the opening game of the 1957-58 season, scoring Tranmere's first goal in a 3-1 win at Chester. He ended his first season with the club as Rovers' leading scorer with 30 goals in 43 League and Cup games including hat-tricks against Bradford Park Avenue (Home 5-0) York City (Home 6-1) and Southport (Away 3-0).

The following season he was joint-top scorer with Tony Rowley with 26 goals in 47 games. He netted a hat-trick in a 3-0 home win over Stockport County and scored four of the club's goals in an 8-1 FA

Cup victory over Bishop Auckland. After a disappointing season in 1959—0, he was back to his best the following season as he once again topped the club's goalscoring charts with 30 goals in 44 games. Included in that total were hat-tricks against Shrewsbury Town (Home 4-2) and Halifax Town (Home 6-2).

Williams who had scored 97 goals in 173 league and Cup games was allowed to leave Prenton Park at the end of the 1960-61 season following an argument with Rovers' manager Walter Galbraith. He joined Plymouth Argyle but his spell at Home Park was brief and six months later he was on the move again, this time to Bristol Rovers where he ended his league career.

WILLIAMS, RAY

Wing-half Ray Williams, the older brother of Keith, joined Rovers straight from school and though he turned professional in 1949, he had to wait until November 1951 before making his first team debut in a 4-2 FA Cup win over Goole Town. Following Johnny Wheeler's departure to Bolton Wanderers, he won a regular place in the Rovers' side and went on to score 16 goals in 214 League and Cup games. His best season for the club in terms of goals scored was 1953-54 when he found the net seven times, occasionally playing at inside or centre forward in an emergency.

By the time his brother Keith had forced his way into the first team, Ray was nearing the end of his career and at the two of them only appeared together in the same Tranmere side on 22 occasions.

At the end of the 1958-59 season, Williams was released and went to live and play in Johannesburg.

WILLIAMSON, STUART

Though he was born in Wallasey, Stuart Williamson moved to Harrogate with his family at a young age and played for the town's Schoolboys team before returning to the Wirral in 1941. After playing in a number of wartime games for Tranmere, he made his league debut for the club in a 3-2 defeat at the hands of Rochdale in October 1946. He was a member of Rovers' league team for the next seven seasons, though he failed to establish himself as a first team regular.

One of the club's most versatile players, he played at full-back, wing-half, centre-forward and outside-left, scoring both goals in a 2-1 home win over Wrexham in his first game at centre-forward.

He went on to score 23 goals in 105 League and Cup games for Tranmere before being allowed to join Swindon Town in the summer of 1953. He appeared in 17 league games for the Robins before hanging up his boots.

WOODWARD, BILLY

Billy Woodward began his career with Manchester United but having failed to make the grade with the Old Trafford club, he joined Tranmere Rovers in the 1933 close season. He made his debut in the opening match of the 1933-34 season and scored a hat-trick in the 5-0 home win over Southport, before going on to end the season with 15 goals in 38 games. Rovers ended the season in seventh place in the Third Division (North) and with Woodward forming a deadly forward partnership with Bunny Bell and Fred Urmson, the club finished sixth in 1934-35 and third in 1935-36.

The goalscoring inside-left scored 44 goals in 110 games during his three seasons at Prenton Park before leaving the club in the summer of 1936 to end his league career with Chesterfield who had just won promotion to the Second Division.

WORST STARTS

The club's worst-ever start to a season was in 1998-99. It took 11 league games to record the first victory of the season, drawing six and losing four of the opening fixtures. The run ended with a 2-1 win at Oxford United on 10 October 1998 when goals from Graham Allen and Gary Jones gave Rovers the points.

WORTHINGTON, FRANK

Frank Worthington was a talented footballer and extrovert character who began his career with Huddersfield Town. After helping the Terriers win the Second Division Championship in 1970, the chance came for him to join Liverpool. A fee of £150,000 had been agreed but a medical examination revealed that he had high blood pressure and Leicester City signed him for a cut-price £80,000.

His elegantly effective centre-forward play was rewarded with an

England call-up and he went on to make eight appearances at full international level. He had scored 72 goals in 210 games for the Foxes when he joined Bolton Wanderers. He became a footballing hero at Burnden Park and soon rediscovered the style which had made him one of the best strikers in the game. In 1977-7 he helped the Wanderers win the Second Division Championship and the following season he ended the campaign with 24 goals to top the First Division goalscoring charts.

After spells with Birmingham City, Leeds United, Sunderland, Southampton and Brighton, he joined Tranmere Rovers as the club's player-manager. He scored on his debut

Frank Worthington, much-travelled striker who had a spell as Tranmere's player-manager.

in a 3-1 defeat at Orient on the opening day of the 1985-86 season and then on his home debut on 23 August he scored a hat-trick in a 6-2 win over Cambridge United. He ended the season as the club's top scorer with 20 goals in 51 games. By the time he lost his job in February 1987, he had scored 24 goals in 74 games. He later played for Preston North End and Stockport County.

One of the game's most gifted and colourful strikers, he made 757 league appearances in a career that saw him approaching his 40th birthday before he left the first-class game.

WRIGHT, JACKIE

Jackie Wright played non-league football for Atherton Collieries and Mossley before joining Blackpool in 1946. Though he was never a first team regular at Bloomfield Road, Wright amassed 167 League and Cup appearances in 13 seasons with the Seasiders. His only goal for the club came in a 4-0 win over Luton Town in September 1956. Wright who won an England 'B' cap whilst with Blackpool was forced to retire through injury and so joined the club's training staff.

In June 1961 he moved to Prenton Park to become Rovers' assistant-manager, stepping up to become boss eight years later when Dave Russell became general manager. He steered Rovers away from relegation in 1969-70 but after the club had come close to the drop again in 1971-72, eventually missing relegation on goal average, Wright was sacked and left the game for good.

'X'

In football 'x' traditionally stands for a draw. The club record for the number of draws in a season was in 1970-71 when they drew 22 of their matches.

XMAS DAY

There was a time when football matches were regularly played on Christmas Day but in recent years the game's authorities have dropped the fixture from their calendar.

Tranmere first played a league game on Christmas Day in 1922 when a goal from Fred Hayes was enough to give Rovers the points at home to Ashington. The north-east side got their revenge on Christmas Day the following year with a 4-2 win over the Rovers, whilst the next two Christmas Day fixtures against Accrington Stanley in 1925 and 1926 saw them win the first encounter 4-3 and Rovers the second 3-2. On Christmas Day 1930, Tranmere beat Rotherham United 6-4 but in 1931, Farewell Watts scored five goals as the Prenton Park club beat Rochdale 9-1. In the first Christmas Day fixture after the Second World War, Harold Atkinson netted a hat-trick in a 5-2 home win over

Lincoln City. Tranmere's last fixture on a Christmas Day was 1957 when they beat Barrow 4-1 at Holker Street with goals from Eglington (2), McDevitt and McDonnell.

YARDLEY, GEORGE

Goalscoring forward George Yardley began his career as a goalkeeper in his native Scotland, playing for East Fife Reserves and Scotland Amateurs before moving to Forfar and Montrose. Desperate to establish himself as a centre-forward, he emigrated to Australia where he played for St George Budapest.

Eventually in 1966 he returned to these shores in an effort to make the grade in league football. Only Rovers' manager Dave Russell was willing to give Yardley a chance and after a month's trial he was given a contract.

He made his debut in a 1-0 defeat at Southport in December 1966 before going on to end the season as the club's top scorer with 16 goals as the Rovers won promotion to the Third Division. In 1967-68 he was again the club's leading scorer with 27 goals including hat-tricks against Colchester United (Home 4-2) and Swindon Town (Home 3-2) and four goals in the 4-1 win over Shrewsbury Town.

A great favourite with the Prenton Park crowd, he damaged his kidneys in Rovers 1-1 draw at Shrewsbury in March 1968 and was advised to quit the game. He returned briefly but after playing at Hartlepool in November 1968 he decided to leave league football and return to Australia.

However, within six months he was back at Prenton Park and in 1969-70 he was again the club's top scorer with 20 goals including another hat-trick in a 3-2 home win over Bury. He finally hung up his boots the following season after scoring 81 goals in 149 games for Rovers.

YEATS, RON

Ron Yeats was described by Bill Shankly his manager at Liverpool as 'the colossus of the defence'. He was signed from Dundee United in

July 1961 for a club record fee of £30,000 and was immediately made captain. Dominant in the air, Yeats was an old- fashioned type of centre-half and in 1965 became the first Liverpool player to lift the FA Cup when they beat Leeds United in the final. He played in 451 games for the Reds, scoring 15 goals. He gained two League Championship medals and in 1966 collected a European Cup Winners' Cup runners-up medal but surprisingly he was only capped twice by Scotland. He left Anfield in December 1971 and moved over the water to Tranmere Rovers as player-assistant-manager later becoming manager.

He made his debut for Rovers in a 3-2 home win over Plymouth Argyle on New Year's Day 1972 and three months later was made player-manager following the departure of Jackie Wright. He took many former Anfield men to Prenton Park including Bobby Graham, Ian St John, Willie Stevenson and Tommy Lawrence. Attendances began to soar as interest in the club was revitalised and though Yeats finished playing at the end of the 1973-74 season after which he had made 110 appearances, he stayed in charge until April 1975 when he was sacked. He returned to Anfield as chief scout in 1986.

YOUNG, TOMMY

Glasgow-born midfielder Tommy Young joined Tranmere Rovers from Falkirk for a fee of £7,000 in June 1972 and made his debut in a 1-0 defeat at Watford on the opening day of the 1972-73 season. Missing just three games in that campaign he was the club's second joint-top scorer with 10 goals, though it was as a maker of goals that he was better known during his five seasons at Prenton Park.

A fiery competitor in the middle of the park, Young scored 29 goals in 193 League and Cup games before being allowed to leave the club on a free transfer at the end of the 1976-77 season. He joined Rotherham United but made just 15 league appearances for the Millmoor club before leaving the first-class game.

YOUNGEST PLAYER

The youngest player to appear in a first team fixture for Tranmere Rovers is Dixie Dean who played in the Third Division (North) match against Rotherham County (Away 1-5) on 12 January 1924 when he was 16 years 355 days old.

Z

ZENITH

Few fans will argue over which moment has been the finest in the club's history. In 1937-38, Tranmere Rovers won their only divisional championship when they won the Third Division (North) title, finishing the season on 56 points, two ahead of Doncaster Rovers.

ZENITH DATA SYSTEMS CUP

Tranmere's first match in the competition during the 1991-92 season saw them play Newcastle United and what a match it was! John Aldridge netted a hat-trick in a 6-6 draw, a match watched by a Prenton Park crowd of just 4,056. In the resultant penalty shoot-out, Rovers won 3-2. In the second round, Aldridge scored another hat-trick in a 5-1 win over Grimsby Town. The former Liverpool striker scored the only goal of the third round as Rovers beat Middlesborough 1-0 at Ayresome Park. Sadly, the Prenton Park club crashed out of the competition in the fourth round, losing 2-0 at Nottingham Forest.

Also of interest:

FOOTBALL & WAR

Gerard Reid

When at war, supporters identify with their 'side' for reasons as diverse as class, religion, and patriotism. Sound familiar? In football, supporters' beliefs can result in conflicts that go far deeper than the actual 'game'. These are the games that this book is about. Chapters include: games where nations were in actual conflict (Argentina v England, and England v Ireland), and even games which were the direct cause of war (Honduras v El Salvador). This is the first book to explore this subject. £6.95

BLEAK AND BLUE:
22 years at the Manchester Academy of Football Farce

Craig Winstanley

An essential read for all Blues fans and for football fans everywhere, Bleak and Blue is a hugely entertaining record of the joys and misery of two decades of the history of Manchester City Football Club. A big book in every way, the author's fanzine-style writing covers all major games in minute detail, relentlessly pursuing a club which could again be a great football club.

"An essential book for all Blues fans; and for all football fans....It's a brilliant read, even if you know nothing – and don't care – about football SOUTH MANCHESTER REPORTER £8.95

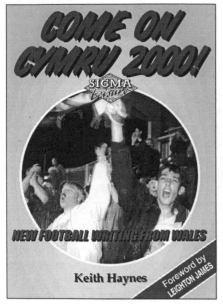

COME ON CYMRU 2000!

Keith Haynes

The original COME ON CYMRU was the first book to give the complete picture of the rivalries between teams and the fervent Welsh pride in their football. This new edition takes Welsh football into the new millennium with the same blend of fanzine-style writing by fans of Welsh football for supporters of football (and Wales!) everywhere. This is how the critics greeted the first edition: "A cracking read, something that Wales has been crying out for, and it's from the fans as well – great stuff!" GERT THOMAS – BBC RADIO WALES

"... Keith Haynes is the Welsh Nick Hornby, you won't put this book down until you've read it from cover to cover." FUTURE MAGAZINE

£6.95

All of our books are available through your local bookseller. In case of difficulty, or for a free catalogue, please contact:

SIGMA LEISURE, 1 SOUTH OAK LANE, WILMSLOW, CHESHIRE SK9 6AR.
Phone: 01625-531035;
Fax: 01625-536800.
E-mail: info@sigmapress.co.uk

Web site: http//www.sigmapress.co.uk

VISA and MASTERCARD welcome.